Les Canadiens

D0967568

LES CANADIENS

a play by Rick Salutin
assist: Ken Dryden

Vancouver, Talonbooks, 1977

copyright © 1977 Rick Salutin

published with assistance from the Canada Council

Talonbooks
201 1019 East Cordova
Vancouver
British Columbia V6A 1M8
Canada

This book was typeset by Linda Gilbert of B.C. Monthly
Typesetting Service, designed by David Robinson and
printed in Canada by Hignell Printing for Talonbooks.

Third printing: June 1992

Text photographs by Anthony Bliss.

Rights to produce *Les Canadiens*, in whole or in part, in any
medium by any group, amateur or professional are retained by
the author and interested persons are requested to apply to
him at Apt. 302, 469 Palmerston Blvd., Toronto, Ontario
M6G 2N9.

The lyrics to the song, "Oh You" on page 99 are by Luce
Guilbeault and Pierre Lenoir. The lyrics to the song, "The
Conquering Canadiens" on page 99 and 101 are by Sebastien
Dhavernas. The lyrics to the song, "The French Lesson" on
pages 131 and 132 are by Pierre Lenoir. All lyrics are used
with permission of their authors.

Canadian Cataloguing in Publication Data

Salutin, Rick, 1942–
    Les Canadiens

    ISBN 0-88922-122-7 pa.

    I. Title.
    PS8587.A4C3   C812'.5'4   C78-002060-X
    PR9199.3.S3C3

Preface

"Would you please send me your autograph . . . a puck . . . your stick . . . your old pads . . . your mask. . . ."

"Can you attend a banquet . . . an opening . . . an auction . . . a birthday party. . . ."

The mail of a hockey player. It comes in a steady stream from September to June, peaking in number as hockey peaks in interest during the Stanley Cup playoffs. Some letters are personal and very special. Most are of a standard form: "Dear Ken, You are the best. Can you please . . ." sent to me and to many other "bests" at the same time, by the same person.

But in late January, 1976, I received a letter quite unlike the other 25,000 or so letters I have received since I began playing with the Canadiens. It was from Maurice Podbrey, Artistic Director of the Centaur Theatre in Montreal. Maurice prefaced his letter, "I'm hoping that this letter doesn't strike you as too way out . . ." and went on to inquire of my interest in collaborating with a director and writer on a play about the Canadiens.

I am at least as Mittyesque as anyone I know and the idea was extremely appealing — so much so that I gave no consideration to the serious problems such an association would almost assuredly create. First, I did not know either Rick Salutin or Guy Sprung, nor did I know their work. Also, since I was a current member of the Canadiens, no matter what my eventual involvement with the production, I most certainly would be closely identified *publicly* with it. Close identification, but little or no control over the final product — that is not a desirable combination.

And while the Canadiens are very much a living and highly visible *institution*, they are above all people: past and present, legends, and those on the way. A proper theatrical treatment of the team and its players would have to provide a dramatic perspective quite different from the spontaneous perspective (non-perspective?) of radio, television and newspapers in which the Canadiens are usually presented. ("Last night, les Canadiens performed brilliantly in turning back . . .") It is not a comfortable feeling to judge one's own friends and associates.

As is sometimes the case, however, not searching out insurmountable obstacles in the first instance led to such obstacles never appearing. They only became frightening "What if's?" in retrospect.

Working with Rick was easy from the beginning. He came to the project without being paralyzed by remotely acquired perceptions of hockey and sports. He was open, interested, and quite simply willing to accept what he found. We had no work format as such. Rather, "work sessions" merely took the form of conversations between friends on a subject of strong mutual interest. It proved a compatible, comfortable and constructive style of working. As time went on, it became evident to me that essentially we shared a common view of the team and its social context. It never occurred to me that the final product could reflect anything other than a perspective with which we would both be happy.

I grew up in Toronto not liking the Canadiens. In the "Who's better?" arguments: Howe or Richard? Sawchuck, Hall or Plante? I always picked Howe, Sawchuck and Hall. But I did not passionately dislike the Canadiens. I did not know them well enough for that. Growing up at that time they were a largely unknown team for most of us outside Quebec. While sometimes tickets could be found for Leaf games against the Bruins or the Red Wings, this was never the case in games against the Canadiens — they were too special. While other teams played in Toronto on Saturdays, the Canadiens played only on Wednesdays, and since it was before the time of Wednesday night hockey telecasts, we never had the chance to see them even on television. They were a team known to us only through the newspapers and on radio. Except in the playoffs, when they appeared on television — and then we saw too much of them. There, they seemed to beat the Leafs all the time. That's why I disliked them, a feeling that only stopped a few years ago when I become a member of the team. How could I have been so misguided all those years? Down with the Leafs!

The Canadiens are very fashionable in these "post-November 15th" days. As perhaps the most visible and accessible symbol of Quebec, they allow people to pour out their feelings toward Quebec through this travelling surrogate, the Canadiens. In Canada, this is manifested largely in expressions of good will (French signs in Maple Leaf Gardens!). In the U.S., where Americans seem able to find deep-rooted political significance in anything, the response is much less emotional and more clinical: it is all seen as a fascinating problem in political science.

But if there is any common view of the Canadiens, it is that they are "more than just a hockey team"; that the team has an impact and imparts a depth of feeling to their public that extends well beyond the result of the last game or the last season. All teams have self-styled fanatical fans ("I haven't missed a home game in thirty years." "That's nothing, I attend all the games." "That's nothing, I . . ."). And the Canadiens have fans all over Canada, in the U.S. and in Europe — not just in Quebec. But these are fanatics like all other sports fanatics, their interest derives from the performance of the team, its style of play, the players, and from the idea of being fanatics about something.

In Quebec though, the effect is different; it is more subtle, pervasive and substantial — yet it is changing. It is that difference and that change that Rick and I have tried to depict in the play.

At a press conference in December, 1976, to promote Jean-Marie Pellerin's book, *Maurice Richard, L'Idole d'un Peuple*, Claude Charron, Québec Minister for Youth, Sport and Recreation commented, "I have the impression that Maurice Richard was one of the original men responsible for giving a special meaning to Québécois life and to have encouraged the élan of the Québec people."

And Richard? At the same press conference he said, "I was just a hockey player. Just a hockey player."

They are both right. The Canadiens — and Richard — are two entities: one to themselves, and one to others. Despite the strong desire we might have to ascribe lofty motives and deep meanings, Richard, his predecessors, and his successors were hockey players, trying to win hockey games, for a hockey team. Nothing else. The players' approach is not marked by a crusading zeal for something "larger." There is no sense of "Let's win one for the embodiment of Quebec's aspirations." From time to time, we may be conscious of the grand historical legacy of the Canadiens, but it is the hockey legacy we feel — being part of a line of players that includes idols of our *own* past — Vezina, Morenz, the Richards, Béliveau, etc.

And despite dramatic appearances to the contrary, the Canadien player of today is very much like his predecessors. The presence of lawyers and agents, the existence of large, no-cut contracts, free agents, expansions, rival leagues, etc., might seem to mock this comment. But these are off-ice diversions. On the ice, the focus is the next face-off, the next save, the next goal — to win. That hasn't changed and that won't change. The excellence of the team remains, and that is our — the players' — focus.

But to others, the Canadiens have changed. In part this is connected to seeing all sport differently. The business of sport has robbed sport of its innocence and specialness, thrusting it into everyday life where it can be judged like everything else.

But in Québec, the change in public perception is more substantial and fundamental. If at one time the Canadiens acted as a focal point for otherwise submerged expressions of nationalistic feeling, they do no more. Claude Charron would never be tempted to describe Guy Lafleur as being "one of the original men responsible for giving a special meaning to Québécois life . . . ." Nor would a future Jean-Marie Pellerin ever write that Lafleur "embodied the spirit of the Québécois." That is only in small part because Richard and Lafleur have markedly different personalities and temperaments. They are both "just hockey players." But their *impact* is defined and determined by others. Others have changed; times are different. It is people and institutions from other parts of Quebec society — politics, the arts, literature — that are now at the focus, and so be it.

I have thoroughly enjoyed working with Rick on this play. Besides the new experience, the opportunity of meeting and working with new and interesting people, it has forced me to take a close look at what has been a major part of my life for the past seven years, and I've come to appreciate "Les Canadiens" even more.

Ken Dryden
Senneville, Quebec
December, 1977

Introduction

It was Guy Sprung who suggested doing a play about the Montreal Canadiens. When I heard about it, it didn't occur to me that I might be the writer. I was, after all, a lifelong Maple Leafs fan. You need an emotional investment to write well about something, and I didn't even *hate* the Canadiens with ferocity. In the aftermath, I *did* become a hot Canadien fan, but even before that, I'd found a way around the problem: make a play not just about the Canadiens, but about Quebec. It was well-known that the Canadiens were "more than just a team" — were the virtual embodiment of Quebec in many ways — and Quebec was a topic I felt very strongly about.

Yet regardless of the outcome, I was delighted. Delighted to be the Canadian playwright someone would go to for a play not about love, or history, or the meaning of life — but about hockey.

Hockey is probably our only universal cultural symbol. It is universal not because every Canadian has played the game — everyone hasn't. But even those who haven't played hockey (most women, for example), nevertheless, relate to hockey. They know what it is, connect it to some context, and have some *feelings* about it. The point is not whether hockey is the world's best, fastest, or most barbaric game; nor whether we are the best in the world at playing it. The

11

point about it is — as Margaret Atwood has said in a similar context about Canadian literature — it is *ours*.

Some aspects of our involvement with hockey may be questionable: the hysterical identification with Canadian teams in international competition, for example. Yet, what does it show — that a country loses control over a hockey team? I would say it shows that we have so little we feel is clearly ours that we develop a — to say the least — very intense relationship with whatever is unequivocally Canadian.

And yet this was to be a play about hockey not in Canada, but in Quebec.

Quebec and Hockey

In English-speaking Canada, hockey sometimes seems to be the virtual assurance that we *have* a culture. That is something never in question in Quebec. Quebec may be ambivalent about its culture and its identity. It may be stiff-necked and proud or, at times, self-hating. But it knows it is. Its problem is not *whether* it is, but how it feels about *what* it is. Accordingly, hockey as a cultural fact in Quebec differs from what it means to *nous autres*.

The point was put to me most eloquently on the banks of the Bow River in Alberta by Red Fisher, sports editor of *The Montreal Star* and visiting lecturer at the Glen Sather Hockey School of Banff.

"What you have to understand," said Red, "is that *ever since the Plains of Abraham, the French people have been number two, but on the ice, they're number one.*"

He went right back to *the* crucial event in the whole history of the French-speaking people of Canada: the conquest of their land by the British Empire over two hundred years ago. Not that they were a free people before then; they were a colony of France. But that was, as it were, *en famille*; it did not have the character of a conquest and subjugation by a foreign power. Since Wolfe's victory though, until today, that sense of being a conquered people, ruled by a foreign power, has remained in Quebec.

This may seem strange to many people outside Quebec (and to some within it as well). Yet in spite of elections, the trappings of modern democracy, etc., that sense of a continuing conquest has not left Quebec. It has been sustained by the experience of real and/or felt oppressions — economic, cultural and political. In 1970, with the proclamation of the War Measures Act and the dispatch of the Canadian Army into Quebec, kids in the streets said to each other, "Regardez les soldats d'Ottawa." *They* felt they'd been (re-)invaded. A very popular show in support of the prisoners held without rights under the Act cast a glance over the entire Quebec past and introduced each scene with the phrase, "Québec, territoire occupée," and then the date, *up to the present.* In this kind of thinking, the actual rule of the British was simply replaced or joined by that of English-speaking Canada (Ottawa) under Confederation, and in recent years, America too has joined the "forces of occupation."

How do people deal with the sense of being perpetually conquered and "occupied?" How do they deal with the humiliation, frustration, anger and defeat? One way taken in Quebec was proclaimed by the Church. Worldly, political power was unimportant to the people of Quebec since they were a uniquely "spiritual" race. Their "vocation" was not to rule, even themselves, but to cultivate religious and intellectual activities. All this was excellent from the viewpoint of the British, or whoever was in charge in Quebec, and it reflects an accommodation reached between the Church hierarchy and those same ruling authorities.

Another route was to refuse to accept subjugation, to fight back. This happened throughout the history of Quebec. In fact, the entire history of French-English relations since the conquest can be seen as an interrupted history of resistance: the revolutionary movement of 1837-38; the Riel rebellions and the support they received in Quebec; the anti-Conscription movements of World Wars I and II; and a host of nationalist and independantist political movements. A continuing resistance, but at the same time, never a victory. They fought, but they did not win.

Here is where Red Fisher's insight comes in. If you fight but don't win — the real battle against the real rulers — then you may try to win elsewhere, in a form where you *are* successful. It is not the same, but at least for the moment you do experience victory over your opponents. Enter les

Canadiens.

Years ago, at a bar in Quebec City, I watched a hockey game on television and marvelled at the frenzied involvement of the patrons. I put to my drinking partner the same question I was later to ask Red Fisher, "How come?" She said, "The Canadiens — they're *us*. Every winter they go south and in the spring they come home conquerors!"

Winners. No team in the history of professional sports, including the New York Yankees, has such a record of winning as do the Montreal Canadiens. The pennants connoting years of Stanley Cup victories are strung like an enormous tapestry the length of the Montreal Forum.

That tradition reached its height with the great Canadien teams of the fifties that won five consecutive Stanley Cups. They were led by Maurice "Rocket" Richard, the embodiment of that spirit in a way no one will ever be again.

His career was contemporaneous with that of Quebec Premier, Maurice Duplessis, under whose rule all forces of political opposition in Quebec were ruthlessly suppressed. Just before the start of the Duplessis era, the spirit of Quebec resistance expressed itself in the great anti-conscription campaign of the Second World War. Almst immediately after Duplessis' death began the incredible series of street demonstrations and mass protest movements that extended right through the sixties and into the seventies. Yet in the entire intermediary period, there was only one comparable event of mass protest: the night in March, 1955, when Canadien fans abandoned the Forum and took to the streets to protest the suspension of Maurice Richard by that walking symbol of Anglo-Canadian authority, NHL president, Clarence Campbell. As Tim Burke, of the *Montreal Gazette* says, "It was the opening shot of the Quiet Revolution."

The Campbell-Richard riot represents the height of the identification of the cause of Quebec with le club de hockey Canadien. Yet it also represents a sort of going beyond the symbol. By spilling out of the Forum and into the streets, the fans seemed to say, "This hockey arena will no longer contain the feelings we have been expressing within it." Such a change is explored in Act Two of *Les Canadiens*.

And yet today, even though things have changed in Quebec (see Note, pp. 15-16), the past remains sufficiently

14

present that *winning* is still what the Canadiens are about:

> I went into the Canadiens' dressing room one Saturday night in 1976 after a game with Boston. The Canadiens had lost. It was the most depressed atmosphere I have ever encountered. I felt like one of those writers who have described being the first Allied soldier into Auschwitz. And yet it was the *only game in forty* that the Canadiens lost at home all season.

> Ken Dryden: "If the Canadiens lost a lot at home, I don't know what the fans would do. I really can't imagine what they would do. It's unthinkable."

> Wayne Thomas: "Nobody kids after a loss. You wouldn't stay long on the team. You can't lose and laugh."

> Dickie Moore: "When you don't win the Cup, it's an awfully long summer in Montreal. Most of the players live here and *everyone* asks, 'What happened?'"

> Many teams give players bonusses for a high team finish in the standings. I've been told players on relatively good teams start receiving increments for every point their team gets over 65. (There are eighty games in a season; teams get two points for a win, one for a tie.) The Canadiens' bonusses don't *start* until 115 points.

> But Red Fisher put it best.

Note — The use of the Canadiens to represent something larger than simply themselves is an example of what Ted Johns has called "the delights of analogy, allegory, and historical parallels" in our theatres. The enjoyment of this kind of "delight" is far more developed in Quebec than it is in the rest of Canada. For example, as Johns points out, Michel Tremblay's play, *Hosanna*, was a great success in

English-speaking Canada, but it was taken almost everywhere as a simple tale of the sexual identity problems of individuals. Whereas, in Quebec, it was enjoyed not only at this straightforward level, but also as an allegory for the identity quest of Quebec society itself.

History of a Script

The Centaur Theatre of Montreal commissioned *Les Canadiens* for their 1976-77 season. Maurice Podbrey, Artistic Director of the Centaur, suggested that Canadiens' goaltender, Ken Dryden, a sometime subscriber and frequent audience member at the theatre, might be willing to help with preparation of the play. This turned out to be an enormous understatement. Ken became a very real collaborator at all stages of development of the script.*

We began with a long meeting at the end of the summer. Ken came armed with pages of notes on being a professional athlete, a hockey star and a Canadien. His observations were very keen, detailed, and tended to be dramatic in form. I had access to something I'd never have been able to gather on my own: the contemporary, day-to-day reality of the institution I was writing about.

A few weeks later I went to Montreal. It was the time of the Canada Cup, the first international series in which Canada iced its best possible hockey team. Ken was not playing in the series due to a recent operation which made him even more accessible than he'd otherwise have been. We toured the Montreal Forum, looked at the dressing room, and met various members of the Forum staff. Then I began a series of interviews based on Ken's suggestions and introductions.

During the next two weeks, or in subsequent visits, I spoke with:

Jean Béliveau, in his office at the Montreal Forum.

---

* Ken's contribution is everywhere, not just in background, but in refining the concept of the play, altering lines, even making suggestions about staging. Yet he gave all this with no check of his own on the final outcome, and should be held in no way responsible for whatever inadequacies appear in the final product.

16

Jacques Beauchamp, editor and sports columnist of *Journal de Montréal*, who absentmindedly flicked cigar ashes into a puck on his desk.

Toe Blake, as he opened his tavern one morning.

Tim Burke of the *Montreal Gazette*.

Dink Carroll, sportswriter emeritus of the *Gazette*.

Al Macneil, former Canadiens' coach, in the seats above the rink after an intrasquad game of Team Canada.

Dickie Moore, at his equipment rental agency, practically on the runway of Dorval airport.

Jacques Plante, at Olympic Stadium, where he was running the food concession during an international bicycle competition.

Henri Richard, in his tavern.

Wayne Thomas, former Canadiens' goalie, in the snack bar at Maple Leaf Gardens.*

I spoke regularly with Ken about what I was learning, what opinions I was forming, what notions for the play were taking shape. Of the many things I came upon, I'd like to mention two.

First, for those who play it, hockey is still a game. I had felt, until this point, that professional hockey must have become something like a business for those on the ice. There were such large sums involved, so many games in a season; they were, after all, professionals; surely, they simply did their jobs more or less consistently, regardless of other,

---

* I found the players I met with articulate and often eloquent, as people tend to be when talking about their work. Many of their words and images found their way into the play. But of all those I spoke with, goaltenders were the most introspective and expressive. It must have something to do with the job.

especially emotional, factors. I was wrong. Players, at least on the Canadiens, feel good when they win, depressed when they lose — in spite of how many dollars they are making per game. It is, to say the least, much more of a game than a business, and much closer to the games we used to play on natural ice after school than to the kind of cool corporate experience I'd anticipated.

The other matter concerns the Rocket, Maurice Richard. He is the only figure who appears in the play who I probably could have talked to, but did not. I intended to meet him, yet as my research went along, a strange thing began to happen. Everyone else talked about the Rocket, and in a unique (though not uniform) way. "It's gotta be Rocket," said Dickie Moore, when I asked him what he would write the play about. "Maurice Richard might be difficult," cautioned someone else. "Ach, Maurice," shrugged his brother, Henri Richard.

I had thought Rocket would be one of the line of Canadien greats in the play: Vezina, Lalonde, Morenz, Richard, Béliveau, Lafleur, but it became unavoidable that the Rocket was *sui generis*. He *was* the Canadiens in some unique way, and the play had to reflect that. It reached the point where I felt that speaking with him would be superfluous. I knew clearly, through others, what he represented for the team and the people of Quebec, and for the purposes of the play, that was sufficient.

I returned to Toronto and started to write.

Then came November 15, 1976. I was well along, somewhere in Act Two, and I'm not sure what I was planning to do with the rest of the play, had the election victory of the Parti Québécois not occurred.

The following night I spoke on the phone with Ken. He said the game at the Forum the previous night, election night, had been a very strange experience. He went on to describe it in the acute manner to which I'd become accustomed. I took notes furiously.

The crowd, he said, was dead. Deader than he'd ever seen at the Forum. They seemed uninterested in the game. So, for that matter, did most of the Canadiens. In fact, the only people in the place who seemed concerned with hockey that night were the hapless St. Louis Blues, who, in spite of the inattention of the Canadiens, still lost the game, 4-2.

But each time an election result was flashed across the message board, everything changed. The crowd awoke. Their excitement mounted with each result, from the early PQ lead in Montreal, to the final declaration that there was a "nouveau gouvernement" in Quebec. The surer the success of the PQ, the more the crowd's ecstasy grew — and the less they cared about the game taking place before them.

As for the players, they had a hard time keeping one eye on the puck and the other on the latest election standings. Moreover, their reaction was opposite to that of the fans. The team — French and English — were known to be over-whelmingly federalist. Former captain Henri Richard had even written a newspaper editorial several days earlier urging people to vote Liberal. The impending victory of the independence party sent them down as much as it lifted the fans up, and yet the Canadiens had for so long been the embodiment of that very nationalism that was now swamping the polls. Even stranger, in the odd emotional mix that was the Forum that night, was the fact that the team was being *ignored*, by their *fans*, in the middle of a *game*, because of an *election*. One thing hockey players in Montreal are not used to is low visibility. They reacted with surprise, dismay, anger, gallows humour ("Take Dryden out and put in Larocque." "Got your passport for the game in Toronto?" "Call me Jean-Pierre Mahovalich."); but, above all, it was, as Ken said, very *confusing* for the young avatars on the ice.

My first thought was: there goes the play. That game meant the cancellation of all I had been building (à la Red Fisher) as the symbolism of les Canadiens. But reflection proved that hasty. For the game of November 15 could be taken as a very natural culmination, fulfillment, transformation, and perhaps a new beginning for that symbolism.

Since the days of the Rocket, Quebec had been changing. Starting with the Quiet Revolution of the early sixties, Quebeckers began to express their sense of national pride and desire for self-assertion in ever more direct ways. It was summed up in the slogan, "Maîtres chez nous" — masters in our own house. Movements arose demanding greater opportunity for Francophones in the economy, and for French language rights. The trade union movements became far more self-confident and, at the same time, both more radical and more nationalistic. Provincial government activity expanded. Francophone cultural activity — novels, theatre, movies, television, music — exploded. And political parties dedicated to the independence of Quebec appeared.

As for the Canadiens, their meaning was changing as the society changed. In the late sixties, Robert Charlebois wore a Canadiens sweater when he performed, but he was a rock singer, not a hockey player. And the more Quebec expressed its national feelings in these *many* ways, the less it had to channel so much of its feeling through its hockey team. This whole process — the repoliticization of a society — culminated on November 15.

It was as though, on that night in the Forum, the people of Quebec finally transferred their need of victory from the shoulders of the hockey team onto their own backs. The Canadiens no longer bore the weight of all that national yearning; they had become, primarily, "just another hockey team." A damn good team, perhaps the best, and one their fans would never cease to adore, but in essence, now a hockey team, and no longer an "army on ice."

That, allowing for the overstatement of someone trying to create a play rather than write history, is what I made of that night.*

The whole of Act Two became The Day of the Game — that very game played at the end of election day. This gave the play an extraordinary timeliness when it was first performed. Within three months of the most dramatic political event in the history of modern Quebec (and perhaps Canada

---

* This is in no way to say that the Canadiens teams of the past *considered* themselves standard-bearers. It is their fans and their society who assigned them the symbolic role. They considered themselves to be hockey players, and that was all. It had to be so, for nothing would be more implausible than a conscious symbol carrying a puck up the ice. This is especially true of the Rocket, who has always maintained he was only playing hockey in spite of many interpretations, recent and ancient, to the contrary. When he attended the opening of *Les Canadiens* in Toronto, he commented that he preferred Act One to Act Two because he "didn't like politics in a play about hockey."

as well) we had a full-length play onstage which incorporated that event as a central structural element. I doubt I will ever again be as timely with a work.

More than that, it gave the play a structure. It would open on the Plains of Abraham with the battlefield turning into a hockey arena, and it would end on November 15, 1976, when a hockey rink is transformed into the site of a great political victory, a sort of conquest of Quebec in reverse.

Act One would be myth: the myth of les Canadiens, standard-bearers of the Quebec spirit; and Act Two would be the demythologization of les Canadiens, and their replacement by the reality of "just a hockey team."

Yet it is neither sad nor tragic because the loss (of the myth) is a gain. Heroic myths of the "Canadiens" ilk serve a purpose because they keep alive the spirit of a people in dark times. But in the end, they are poor solutions to real problems. If the problem is political, then the solution must be political, not symbolic. Nor have you really "lost" the Canadiens. On the contrary, they are now free to be what they really are: not national saviors, but a great team and beloved institution.

Brecht said, "Unhappy is the nation that has no heroes." This could well stand as the motto for Act One. But then he added, "No. Unhappy is the nation that *needs* a hero." And this could be the motto for Act Two, expressing the strength to divest oneself of myths, face reality, and seek out real rather than symbolic solutions.

The structure (from myth to reality) was also the theme.

The Second Production

The second production of *Les Canadiens* was done in October, 1977, at Toronto Workshop Productions. For the most part, it is the script of this latter production which is reproduced here. For this production, Act One remained largely as it had been. Act Two, however, was rewritten. A number of scenes were eliminated; others were lengthened or substantially altered. A new character appeared, a fictional member of the current Canadiens named Dave Kirk. He played foward, and replaced a Ken Dryden character from the earlier script.

21

This represented a move away from the "documentary" style to a more traditionally "dramatic" mode: unity around a central character and his "problem." We were moving away in time from the impact of the event, (The Day of the Game) and a more sculpted, fictionalized approach seemed appropriate.

Something else occurred in the second production. I would say that the play found its audience.

The Montreal audiences at the Centaur had responded very warmly to the play, partly because of the incredible love of all Montrealers for their hockey team. Still, there was something in the point of view of the play not directly useful to them. The scattering of Francophones who came each night appreciated the sympathy of the play toward Quebec nationalism particularly since it was coming from an Anglophone source — yet in the end, it was nothing new to them. Their own writers have taken this point of view for years.

The Montreal Anglophones — the vast majority of our audience there — had varied reactions, but I think it would be right to say that the play did not really address their particular problem, which is: becoming a minority. For years the Anglophones of Quebec have identified with the rest of Canada and assumed thereby the sense of being a majority. Now, whether independence actually comes to Quebec or not, they are faced with the need of making the transition from majority to minority.

But English-speaking Canadians outside of Quebec are not faced with any such drastic alteration in their life circumstances as a result of recent events. Their problem regarding Quebec is simpler: what to make of it all — of the election, and of the entire train of events in Quebec over the last seventeen years.

In high school history class, I recall that Quebec always seemed to be a trouble-maker. Those French Canadians were fractious, rambunctious — the fly in the ointment of Canadian history (or, as a McGill University professor put it less quaintly during World War II, "cockroaches in the kitchen of Canada"). Much of the initial commentary in English-speaking Canada after the PQ victory was an extension of that approach: there were a bunch of trouble-makers up there in the Parti Québécois, duping their own people and

22

intent on messing things up for the rest of us. It was a mean-spirited reponse, and not very historically relevant either.

I hope *Les Canadiens* achieves a different, non-hysterical response to those events. To begin with, no one should be *surprised*. The election of the PQ is one more in a long chain of national self-assertions by the people of Quebec that extends through the length of their history. Beyond that, one can be heartened at the sight of a people standing up for their dignity and asserting themselves.* And, beyond that, I think one can even draw some inspiration: if the people of Quebec can stand up for themselves, then perhaps the rest of us in Canada can do the same for ourselves.

There was great confusion in English-speaking Canada in the wake of the November 15 election. It was not unlike the confusion of the players on the ice at the Forum that night. Many who cared about the future of the country felt it was being broken apart. Yet it was hard not to admire the concern for *their* country of those very people who seemed to be breaking Canada apart. And those politicians who previously seemed content to preside over the disintegration of Canada by selling it off or letting it drift, those very politicians, suddenly proclaimed themselves the *saviours* of Canada.

But in the aftermath, some clarity started to emerge. What at first seemed a threat could be taken as a challenge. Not only a challenge, but possibly an opportunity. An opportunity for those of us outside Quebec to re-think what kind of country *we* want, with or without Quebec — and, in the urgency of crisis, to re-shape what is obsolete or undesirable. I hope *Les Canadiens* can aid in that process of clarification for those in audiences outside Quebec, not insofar as they are theatre-goers, but insofar as they are Canadians.

What a season! Montreal won the Stanley Cup; the people of Quebec reversed a historical verdict; and, on another level

---

* I hope it is clear that the hopefulness of the play hangs not on the PQ, nor on the new government of Quebec, much less on any particular policies of that government, past or future; it is a hopefulness based on the act of self-respect by the *people of Quebec* which the election represented.

to be sure, we made *Les Canadiens*. What a hell of a season it was!

Rick Salutin
Toronto, Ontario
December, 1977

"The whole thing about being a Canadian is that you root all winter *against* the Montreal Canadiens, because they're *French*, and then comes the Stanley Cup playoffs, and you root *for* them because they're *Canadian* and they're playing against *American* teams!"

Eric Peterson
Actor in the Montreal production
of *Les Canadiens*

"It was a dream, and everything I dreamed came true. Now my dream is finished. That's a new life for me. Because what I do now, what I keep on doing, is something I never dreamed of."

Henri Richard

Les Canadiens was commissioned by and first performed at Centaur Theatre in Montreal, Quebec, on February 10, 1977, with the following cast: Raymond Belisle, Sebastien Dhavernas, Luce Guilbeault, Ray Landry, Pierre Lenoir, Eric Peterson and Michael Rudder.

Directed by Guy Sprung
Designed by Astrid Janson
Lighting by Steven Hawkins

Les Canadiens was also performed at Toronto Workshop Productions in Toronto, Ontario, on October 20, 1977, with the following cast: Raymond Belisle, Jeff Braunstein, Suzette Couture, Sebastien Dhavernas, Len Doncheff, Bill Lake, Pierre Lenoir and Johnathan Welsh.

Directed by George Luscombe
Designed by Astrid Janson
Lighting by Simon Reeve

The author wishes to thank members of the cast in both productions who aided in finalizing the script.

Les Canadiens was also performed at The Arts Club Theatre in Vancouver, B.C., on April 20, 1978, with the following cast: Guy Bannerman, Jon Bryden, Lally Cadeau, David Crowley, Michael Fawkes, Andy Maton, Murray Ord, Harvey Stenson and Ray Whelan.

Directed by Brian Richmond
Designed by Alison Green
Lighting by Marsha Sibthorpe

Act One
Survival

*The theatre is the Montreal Forum. The stage
is the ice. There are stands, a time clock, a
broadcast booth and an electronic message
board. The PLAYERS are finishing their
warm-up on the ice as the crowd-audience
enters. The PLAYERS leave the ice for their
final pre-game preparations. The Forum
ORGANIST performs an overture to the
game. The USHERS and VENDORS do their
appointed tasks.*

ANNOUNCER: *from the broadcast booth, à la Claude
Mouton* Bonsoir mesdames et messieurs et bienvenus
au Forum de Montréal. Good evening ladies and
gentlemen and welcome to the Montreal Forum.
Le match de ce soir ... tonight's game ... Les
Canadiens contre tous et chacun ... the Canadiens
against all comers. Et maintenant veuillez accueillir
... and now please welcome ... nos Canadiens!

*The PLAYERS enter to the cheering of the
crowd and the strains of "Les Canadiens sont
là." The game begins. The time clock starts at*

27

20:00 and clicks the seconds downward. A fight breaks out. Suddenly, the situation is transformed. The time clock has reached 17:59 and we are on the Plains of Abraham. The PLAYERS have become SOLDIERS. The message board reads: "The Conquerors and the Conquered." The ORGANIST plays "Rule Britannia."

WOLFE:

> We've won. The day is ours. One empire goes. Another comes.

AIDE:

> The battle is continuing, sir. On the east flank. At the river.

WOLFE:

> It will continue a while yet. On one flank or another.

AIDE:

> Yes, sir. Webb and Burton are still in reserve.

WOLFE:

> And yet we've won. For now we make the rules. Montcalm, you can't cross here. You can't retreat there. Ah-ha, no supplies by that route. You see? The game is ours.

AIDE:

> Sir, the Charles Bridge . . .

WOLFE:

> Give me Gray.

AIDE:

> The poetry, sir?

WOLFE:

> A time to act and a time to reflect on action.

AIDE:

  There's heavy fighting at the bridge, sir.

WOLFE:

  See to it then!

AIDE:

  Sir!

  The AIDE starts off.

WOLFE:

  The Elegy!

  The AIDE gives him a volume of poetry.
  He exits. WOLFE begins to read.

  Now fades the glimmering landscape on the sight,
  And all the air a solemn stillness holds. . . .

  A British SOLDIER enters pursuing a retreating
  French FARMER.

SOLDIER:

  Halt!

  A SECOND SOLDIER enters. He cuts off the
  FARMER's retreat.

SECOND SOLDIER:

  Ho!

WOLFE:

  Montcalm, I salute your hopeless cause. British
  soldiers against Canadian peasants.

  The SOLDIERS dispatch the FARMER.

FARMER:

  Aggghhhh! Viarge!

29

WOLFE: *reading*
> Oft did the harvest to their sickle yield,
> Their furrows oft the stubborn glebe has broke,
> How jocund did they drive their team afield!
> How bow'd the woods beneath their sturdy stroke!

The SOLDIERS are ransacking the fallen body.

FIRST SOLDIER:
> There's fuck-all.

SECOND SOLDIER:
> He's got a musket.

FIRST SOLDIER:
> I'll take it.

SECOND SOLDIER:
> Like hell.

WOLFE:
> Gentlemen!

BOTH SOLDIERS:
> General Wolfe!

WOLFE:
> In victory, magnanimity!

FIRST SOLDIER:
> What, General?

WOLFE:
> I understand we are still engaged by the enemy.
> Elsewhere on this field.

The SOLDIERS exit.

FARMER:
> Maudits Anglais!

WOLFE:
>I do it gladly.

>*He returns to his poetry.*

>Let not ambition mock your useful toil,
>Your homely joys and destiny obscure;
>Nor grandeur hear with a disdainful smile
>The short and simple annals of you poor . . . Canadians.

>>*A crack from a rifle is heard. The FARMER
>>has shot WOLFE with his musket. WOLFE
>>falls. The FARMER'S SON enters.*

FARMER'S SON:
>Papa, Papa. Maman t'attend à la maison.

>>*Elsewhere on the field, the FARMER'S WIFE
>>enters.*

FARMER'S WIFE:
>Gérard, I brought more powder.

>>*Wolfe's AIDE re-enters.*

AIDE:
>We've opened the bridge, sir. Your orders . . .

WOLFE:
>Help me die in peace.

AIDE:
>General!

>>*He kneels to help WOLFE. The PLAYERS
>>begin to construct the familiar historical tableau.*

FARMER'S WIFE:
>What a mess!

WOLFE:
>Read!

FARMER'S WIFE:
>Maudits Anglais!

AIDE: *reading*
>The boast of heraldry, the pomp of power,
>And all that beauty, all that wealth e'er gave,
>Awaits alike th' inevitable hour:
>The paths of glory lead but to the grave.

FARMER:
>Ah, viarge.

WOLFE:
>I'd rather have written those lines than won this battle.

FARMER'S SON:
>Papa?

WOLFE:
>Or any line that men remember.

FARMER'S WIFE:
>Ils sont jamais satisfait. L'Europe, L'Amérique. Maintenant le Canada.

FARMER:
>Ici.

A British SOLDIER enters.

SOLDIER:
>They run! Sir, they run!

AIDE:
>Sssh.

FARMER:
Ici.

The FARMER'S SON hears him.

WOLFE:
Who runs?

AIDE:
You've won, sir.

WOLFE:
I knew that.

FARMER'S WIFE:
Cochons anglais!

AIDE:
They can't prevent it.

WOLFE: *sensing a memorable line*
Prevent it?

AIDE:
Quebec is ours.

WOLFE:
I die . . .

Rhyming with "prevent it."

. . . contented.

The lights fade on the tableau.

FARMER'S WIFE:
Gérard, où es-tu? You never could shoot.

FARMER'S SON: *to the FARMER*
T'es vivant?

FARMER:

No, I'm pretending to talk so they don't bury me.

FARMER'S SON:

Maudit P'pa. I'll drag you.

FARMER:

Non. Laisse-moi!

FARMER'S WIFE:

Hey!

FARMER'S SON:

Il est ici.

FARMER'S WIFE:

Is he alive?

FARMER'S SON:

Y dit qu' oui.

FARMER'S WIFE:

Well, what are you waiting for?

She comes over to where they are.

FARMER'S SON:

He doesn't want to come.

FARMER'S WIFE:

What? Look out. Take an arm.

FARMER:

Laisse-moi!

FARMER'S WIFE:

Crisse! Pourquoi?

FARMER:

I like it.

FARMER'S WIFE:
Quoi?

FARMER:
You think you gotta be a general to die in battle?

FARMER'S WIFE:
Did you get the General? That was good.

FARMER:
You think you gotta be French or English to die in a battle?

FARMER'S WIFE:
Come on, we've got the farm. You want the English to get the crops?

FARMER:
Fuck off!

Turning to his SON.

You too!

FARMER'S SON:
Alright, alright, let the English have him.

FARMER'S WIFE:
No!

Speaking to her SON.

You get back.

Speaking to the FARMER.

You shut up. You gonna let them win? Just like that?

FARMER'S SON: *leaving, but upset*
The hell with him.

FARMER: *to his SON*
    Hey.

FARMER'S SON:
    Quoi?

FARMER:
    Peux-tu l'attraper?

FARMER'S WIFE:
    Tabarnac!

FARMER'S SON:
    Yeah, sure, I can catch.

FARMER'S WIFE:
    Y sont fous.

FARMER:
    They want our guns and they want our hands.
    They're not getting mine.

    He strains to rise and recite the following lines
    from "In Flander's Fields," which are written
    in English and French on the wall of the dressing
    room of the Montreal Canadiens at the Forum.

    To you from failing hands we throw the torch,
    Be yours to hold it high.

FARMER'S SON:
    Maudit P'pa, that sounds like something an
    Englishman would say.

FARMER'S WIFE:
    We've really lost now.

WOLFE: *a last gasp*
    A line they'll remember.

FARMER:
Tiens.

With his last breath, he throws his rifle to his SON. As his SON catches it, it turns into a hockey stick. The FARMER'S SON does not know what to do with it. The lights fade on him. WOLFE, his AIDE and his SOLDIERS exit. The FARMER and the FARMER'S WIFE exit.

The time clock reads 18:67. The message board reads: "From Sea to Sea." The scene is an outdoor skating rink. Present and skating are JOHN A. MACDONALD and SIR EDWARD WATKIN, a British financier. The FARMER'S SON is also present with his hockey stick. He is gradually discovering its uses and growing more adept with it.

WATKIN:
I assure you, Macdonald, that the Directors of the Grand Trunk would not have sent me here all the way from London, were they not certain a way to restore the health of the railroad could be found.

The FARMER'S SON with his hockey stick cuts past them.

MACDONALD:
Careful, Sir Edward.

WATKIN:
Here, what's this?

MACDONALD:
And your solution?

WATKIN:
Expansion, by God. Build the line from the Atlantic to the Pacific. Unify your separate colonial governments into one national system large enough to

guarantee the necessary loans . . . and the investment
is saved!

MACDONALD:
   Brilliant! Of course.

WATKIN:
   One country. Call it what you want.

MACDONALD:
   Bit dodgey perhaps.

WATKIN:
   You're thinking of those rowdy Quebeckers.

MACDONALD:
   On the other hand, they might be pleased.
   Government of their own again. For local matters
   only. Education and the like.

   The RINK OWNER enters, a smalltime
   businessman.

RINK OWNER:
   Clear the ice. Time's up, gentlemen.

WATKIN:
   Time, Macdonald? I thought the party paid for this
   place.

MACDONALD:
   Only till now. They've rented it to the regiment.

WATKIN:
   Our regiment? For what?

RINK OWNER:
   Hockey.

WATKIN:
   Hockey?

MACDONALD:
Ice hockey. It's their recreation.

An English REGIMENT enters. They skate and play very stiffly. They use a ball which keeps hopping over their sticks.

WATKIN:
Ice hockey? As in field hockey? Played on ice instead of a field. How exotic!

MACDONALD:
You'll want to move the capital, I suppose.

WATKIN:
You decide.

MACDONALD:
And what to call it?

WATKIN:
Must be hundreds out there. Berserkers eh wot?

RINK OWNER:
There are no rules. Only scores.

WATKIN: *with admiration*
How basic.

MACDONALD:
Not a confederacy. Not with the war in the States.

He is getting caught up in the game.

Not a federation.

WATKIN:
Come along, Macdonald. I'm sure something can be made of this country that will last.

WATKIN exits.

RINK OWNER:
Collecting your skates, sir?

MACDONALD:
Certainly not a republic. Yes, of course. Not quite
a monarchy.

RINK OWNER:
You have to take them off first.

MACDONALD: *sitting down in the stands*
What? Oh, just glancing at the game while I remove
them.

RINK OWNER:
Lots do.

MACDONALD:
Do you mind?

RINK OWNER:
Doesn't cost a cent.

MACDONALD:
Aha.

> *He gives the RINK OWNER some money.*

Right.

RINK OWNER:
You know, sometimes I think I could sell tickets to
this thing.

MACDONALD:
Pay? To watch others play?

> *The FARMER'S SON grabs the ball from the*
> *REGIMENT and, by slicing off two parallel*
> *segments, invents the puck. It no longer hops*

over a stick. He proudly hands the puck back to the REGIMENT.

The time clock reads 18:85. The message board reads: "Métis Rebels Proclaim New Nation in West." An older MACDONALD sits in the stands still watching the game.

Oh, Watkin, it seemed like a good idea at the time. Give them their own little province and leave the nation building to us. And now they want the whole of the West. Our West. We haven't even finished your railroad and the whole new country's disintegrating. Nova Scotia threatening to leave yet again. British Columbia losing patience. And the West in open revolt. Halfbreeds and Frenchmen and crazy-like-a-fox Riel. Hang Louis Riel!

The FARMER'S SON has discovered how to raise the puck. He is getting better and better at it as MACDONALD continues to speak.

Perhaps. The blessed deed that might save the country. A transcontinental symbol that doesn't need rails. National Unity at last. Canadians cheering the just deed at the end of a rope in every province from sea to sea. Except Quebec. Very unpopular in Quebec. They'll start talking about their "national" party again. Well, it'll hurt the Liberals as much as us. . . .

The MOTHER of the FARMER'S SON enters. She is and is not the same woman that we saw on the Plains of Abraham. She addresses her SON.

MOTHER:
So, this is it? The place you can't stay away from? So, you're never at home, you're never in school, you're never at church.

FARMER'S SON:
    Hi, M'man.

MOTHER:
    Alright, explain to me. What happens here? That's
    more important than helping your people, or your
    family, or yourself even? What is this place?

FARMER'S SON:
    It's a hockey rink.

MOTHER:
    Yes, I can see. Ice. And what happens here?

FARMER'S SON:
    Well, the people come. When they have the time.
    They get on the ice. There's the puck. The goals.
    They go from one end to the other. The idea is to
    get the puck in the goal.

        *He starts to demonstrate, in his own style,
        to the discomfiture of the stiff Anglo players
        of the REGIMENT.*

    But you can pass it, you see. Or, if the other side
    thinks you're going one way, you can go the other.
    Zip, zip, zip. Or flip it up over their sticks.

MOTHER:
    Games. That's right, isn't it? They play games!

FARMER'S SON:
    Yeah, it's a game.

MOTHER:
    I want to know, so what? So what, they play a game?
    So what?

FARMER'S SON:
    I dunno.

MOTHER:

> Is it important? Am I missing something? Is there
> something else here?

FARMER'S SON:

> I guess not.

MOTHER:

> You got no pride? You know what they're doing to
> our people in the West? You care? What's this got to
> do with us? Show me . . . so I'll understand . . . why
> a Canayen . . . a young, strong Canayen . . . in times
> like this . . . slides on ice! Come, explain it to me.
> When you can.

> *She exits.*

> *MACDONALD has been weighing things while
> observing this confrontation.*

MACDONALD:

> Oh, it'll tear the country apart. So be it. It's the only
> way to keep us together. Riel must swing!

> *Wham! The FARMER'S SON unleashes a
> vicious slapshot in MACDONALD's direction.
> The REGIMENT turns on him. MACDONALD
> exits.*

REGIMENT:

> Murderer! Degenerate! Halfbreed! Avenge the death
> of Thomas Scott! Fire and bloodshed! And Canada
> First!

> *The REGIMENT runs the FARMER'S SON off
> the ice, leaving the RINK OWNER behind.*

> *The time clock reads 19:09. The message
> board reads: "Business Trusts Threaten Free
> Competition."*

RINK OWNER:
George, George, where have you been?

The FARMER'S SON re-enters.

FARMER'S SON:
Delivering Eaton's catalogues.

RINK OWNER:
Get out there and clean up. We gotta do something with this place.

J. AMBROSE O'BRIEN, millionaire sportsman, enters.

O'BRIEN:
Why wasn't Jesus Christ born in Quebec?

FARMER'S SON:
Fifteen cents admission, sir.

RINK OWNER:
I don't know. Why wasn't Jesus Christ born in Quebec?

FARMER'S SON:
Fifteen cents admission to get in.

O'BRIEN:
Because they couldn't find three wise men and a virgin!

The two men laugh uproariously.

RINK OWNER:
J. Ambrose O'Brien, the old prospector.

O'BRIEN:
Not anymore. I struck it rich up Cobalt way.

RINK OWNER:
> What're you doing down here?

O'BRIEN:
> Looking for a game.

RINK OWNER:
> Where's your skates?

> *More hilarity. The FARMER'S SON is unamused.*

O'BRIEN:
> I own my own teams now. Three of them. Parked outside. We killed off all the opposition in North Ontario, so we came south.

RINK OWNER:
> I got a team. Montreal Wanderers. They're just sitting around.

O'BRIEN:
> Hey, you and me can be a league.

RINK OWNER:
> A what?

O'BRIEN:
> A league. We'll play each other. Have standings. Give some kind of award.

RINK OWNER:
> I got an award around here somewhere.

> *Speaking to the FARMER'S SON.*

> Hey, where's that cup?

O'BRIEN:
> We'll call it . . . the National Hockey League.

The ORGANIST plays the "Hockey Night in Canada" theme.

Speaking to the FARMER'S SON.

Boy, you like hockey? We're starting a new league.

FARMER'S SON:
More English teams.

O'BRIEN:
Not English teams. Hockey teams. Hockey knows no language.

Speaking to the RINK OWNER.

What's with him?

RINK OWNER:
They're like that.

O'BRIEN: *to the FARMER'S SON*
Doesn't your Frenchman play hockey?

FARMER'S SON:
For the English.

O'BRIEN:
You don't like the English?

FARMER'S SON: *handing him a bedraggled Stanley Cup*
Here's your cup.

O'BRIEN:
I want a team here. A French team.

RINK OWNER:
A French team? You don't know what you're letting the lid off. The French hate the English. They'd go wild. . . . It might work.

O'BRIEN starts to exit.

Hey, where you going?

O'BRIEN:
Buy some Frenchmen for the Montreal . . .
Frenchmen?

RINK OWNER:
Sounds English.

O'BRIEN:
Trappers? Peasants? Missionaries? The Montreal
Missionaries!

RINK OWNER:
Canadiens.

O'BRIEN:
Canadians?

RINK OWNER:
Like *they* say it. Ca-na-dyens.

O'BRIEN:
The Ca-na-dyens.

RINK OWNER:
Les Canadiens.

O'BRIEN:
Aw, what's in a name? Hey, boy, you play hockey?
See me later.

> *The RINK OWNER and O'BRIEN exit. The
> FARMER'S SON remains behind. He sings,
> tentatively at first, the theme song of Les
> Canadiens.*

FARMER'S SON:
>Hot-la, hot-la, hot-la,
>Les Canadiens, les Canadiens,
>Hot-la, hot-la, hot-la,
>Les Canadiens sont là.

>>*He repeats the song, more confidently, and is about to finish it off, when his MOTHER interrupts.*

MOTHER:
>Georges, qu'est-ce que tu fais là maintenant? Don't tell me it's different this time?

FARMER'S SON:
>Yeah, I play hockey!

>>*The MOTHER exits as he finishes the last line of the song.*

>Les Canadiens sont là!

>>*The time clock reads 19:10. The message board reads: "500,000 Quebeckers Move to U.S.A. in Search for Jobs."*

>>*The original Canadiens burst onto the ice at the Old Victoria Rink. They are announced through a megaphone. The game is against the Wanderers and both English and French FANS are in the stands. The Canadiens already show the grace, élan and reckless speed for which they became famous.*

ANNOUNCER: *from the broadcast booth*
>Bonsoir mesdames et messieurs, et pour les Canadiens, Jacques Laviolette!

>>*The PLAYERS come forward on the ice as their names are called.*

FRENCH FAN:
> Yayyyyy!

ENGLISH FAN:
> Must be his brother.

ANNOUNCER:
> Louis Berlinguette.

FRENCH FAN:
> Yayyyyyy!

ENGLISH FAN:
> Hey, what's going on?

ANNOUNCER:
> Bertrand Corbeau.

FRENCH FAN:
> Yayyyyyy!

ENGLISH FAN:
> They can't *all* be his brother.

ANNOUNCER:
> Didier Pitre.

FRENCH FAN:
> Yayyyyyy!

ENGLISH FAN:
> They're cheering because of the names!

ANNOUNCER:
> Jacques Fournier.

FRENCH FAN:
> Yayyyyyy!

ENGLISH FAN:
>Looniest thing I ever saw. Hockey team of
>Frenchmen!

ANNOUNCER:
>Newsy Lalonde.

FRENCH FAN:
>Yayyyyyy!

ENGLISH FAN:
>Everyone knows your Frenchmen aren't your
>physical types. They're more spiritual. Small too.

ANNOUNCER:
>Sylvio Mantha.

>*MANTHA is massive.*

FRENCH FAN:
>Yayyyyyy!

ENGLISH FAN:
>Wanderers'll take 'em. My team. Good English stock.

ANNOUNCER:
>Georges Vezina.

>*It is the FARMER'S SON with his stick. He has
>now become VEZINA, the greatest goaltender
>of all time.*

FRENCH FAN:
>Yayyyyyy!

ENGLISH FAN:
>At last, here they come now. Hurrayyyy Wanderers!
>Go get 'em, boys. Massacre those peasoupers.

>*The Wanderers are a classic English team — big,*

beefy, clunky. They are perfect stereotyped foils to the stereotyped Gallicity of the Canadiens.

They face VEZINA time and time again, but they cannot get the puck past him into the net.

Finish him off and let's go home early. Put the puck behind that hayseed. Stuff it down his throat. Give him a haircut. Stick him in the gut. What're you waiting for?

FRENCH FAN:
Yayyyyyy!

ENGLISH FAN:
Very excitable, your Frenchman. Emotional. Hasn't got much in his life to hoot about. It's all pretty boring. Work, family. So he lets it out here. Hey, knock that Frenchie on his can!

The Wanderers assault VEZINA and knock him down.

Two bucks fine for going down, Vezina. We don't play that way.

VEZINA continues to hold them off.

'Course, that goalie, gotta admit he's not completely useless. Musta learned it down in Verdun.

The time clock advances to 19:16. The message board reads: "Union Government Pledges Full Support to Empire. Laurier Refuses to Join."

And they did win a Stanley Cup. Know why? 'Cause all the English boys went off to fight the war!

The MOTHER re-enters. Again, she is and is not the same woman as before.

MOTHER:

> The maudits Anglais! They're running all over us
> again.

ENGLISH FAN:

> Stay on your feet, Vezina, or you're out. You play
> by the rules!

MOTHER:

> Your father's gone off to hide in the woods and
> you've gone again to your goddamned game!

ENGLISH FAN:

> Whole battalions full of great hockey shooters. The
> 228th. Northern Fusiliers. Ordered overseas. And
> off they went. While your "Canadiens" keep playing
> hockey like Christian civilization isn't even on the
> brink. . . .

MOTHER:

> Like always, the men. These ones go off to fight the
> war. These ones go off to hide so they don't have to
> fight the war. These ones just go off. To the hockey
> rink.

ENGLISH FAN:

> We'll beat 'em anyway. C'mon, boys.

MOTHER:

> What about us? What about the farm? What about
> Québec?

> *The Wanderers are exiting, demoralized by*
> *VEZINA and called by the far-off war.*

ENGLISH FAN:

> Hey, where you guys going? You can't pack up.
> You're my team, my boys, you can't fold. Bloody
> war. Ruin everything before it ends. If it ends. I'm
> not gonna stay and watch a bunch of Frenchmen
> butcher hockey.

He exits.

MOTHER:

You go off to your wars and your games and you forget everything else. And you know what? I can't do that!

FRENCH FAN:

Hey, maudits Anglais, come back. It's no fun without you buggers to beat.

He exits.

MOTHER:

I can't fight in your goddamned wars and I can't play in your goddamned games! But I'm going to save the next one. He may grow up crazy like his father and his brothers, but it won't be for hockey. I'll save him from hockey!

She exits.

VEZINA is left alone on the ice. He is worn down by the battle and near the end of his great career.

The time clock reads 19:21.

O'BRIEN re-enters.

O'BRIEN:

Rules, rules, rules. The whole game's got sissified. I'm gonna get rid of these teams. Who wants to buy a hockey team?

LEO DANDURAND enters, a Montreal man-about-town and a small scale operator. He is reading a racing form.

Hey, you, wanta team?

DANDURAND:
> Pacers or racers?

O'BRIEN:
> Huh?

DANDURAND:
> Your horses.

O'BRIEN:
> Are you from the track?

DANDURAND:
> Is the Pope Catholic?

O'BRIEN:
> What?

DANDURAND:
> Is Léo Dandurand from the track?

O'BRIEN:
> Leo, lookit here.

> *He displays VEZINA as if he were a thorough-bred.*

DANDURAND:
> Pas mal.

O'BRIEN:
> Hey, that's merchandise. What'll you gimme?

DANDURAND:
> Whatever I've got. $10,000.00.

O'BRIEN:
> That's ridiculous! Sold!

> *They exit.*

The message board reads: "$10,000.00."

VEZINA, still alone on the ice, looks for someone that he can pass his stick to. There is no one.

ANNOUNCER: *from the broadcast booth*
Your attention please. Now arriving on Platform 12. Train from Windsor, London, Toronto, Kingston and . . . Stratford.

VEZINA turns away.

The time clock reads 19:23. The message board reads: "Ontario Passes Quebec in Population, Wealth."

We are in the Windsor Station in Montreal and HOWIE MORENZ, a farmboy from Stratford, Ontario, has just got off the train. He is rehearsing a speech.

MORENZ:
My Dad and I feel. . . . I appreciate this, I do. . . . Here's your money, Mr. Dandurand. I'm sure you'll be glad to get it back. Cripes, $850.00! I got this good job in Stratford and Dad says that jobs at the CNR don't grow on trees, not even in the fruitbelt. Aw . . . my pals, my girl. . . . The *Toronto Star* says it's a papal plot to steal me away from my people and the Orange Lodge had a special convocation . . . and Reverend Peachtree says Montreal's the devil's den. Geez, what if I like it? Shit, Mr. Dandurand, I'm not very good. I'm saving you money. Toronto'd be bad, but Montreal. . . . It's like going overseas. I don't even speak French. I wouldn't know if you were telling me to shoot or get off the ice. Yeah. That's good. Mr. Dandurand, believe it or not, I don't even talk a word. . . . *He*'s not gonna know what I'm telling him. Shit. Monsyoor Dandoorand. Oh, hell,

Montreal. Sin. Temptation. The devil. How do you
even know him?

DANDURAND re-enters.

DANDURAND:
Howie?

MORENZ:
Who's asking?

DANDURAND:
Howie Morenz. I knew it. I'm Léo Dandurand.

MORENZ:
Knew it how?

DANDURAND:
You fit in.

MORENZ:
Me? Here?

DANDURAND:
Like the fizz in a phosphate. Well, what do you think?

MORENZ:
About what?

DANDURAND:
Our little town.

MORENZ:
Oh, I'm okay. I mean, it's okay. You know, I was
sure you'd be one of those peasoupers.

DANDURAND does not respond to this remark.

Ah, Mr. Dandurand, I've got something here to give
you. . . .

DANDURAND: *avoiding the bonus cheque in MORENZ's hand* I'll take your bags. Come on.

They enter the Montreal Forum.

MORENZ:
It's my bonus cheque. See, my Dad and my girlfriend says . . . the Reverend back home . . . all my pals . . .

He surveys the Forum and is wide-eyed.

They wouldn't even believe this place! It's gigantic!

DANDURAND:
Missing home already?

MORENZ:
Oh, yeah. Stratford. Great town.

They view the Forum from the top of the stands.

DANDURAND:
Behold, the Montreal Forum, the eighth wonder of the world.

MORENZ:
You see so much.

DANDURAND:
You know, while you're here I think you should see some other things as well. The Mountain! It's not a real mountain, but everyone calls it *the* mountain, as though it's the only one in the world.

MORENZ:
I've been up the Niagara Escarpment. It's pretty high.

DANDURAND:
You can see where the two rivers come together. The Ottawa . . .

MORENZ:
>   From Ontario.

DANDURAND:
>   And the St. Laurent.

MORENZ:
>   Makes you feel poetic . . .

>   *A RINK ATTENDANT enters.*

RINK ATTENDANT:
>   Franchement, Léo, je trouve que tu exagères.

DANDURAND:
>   J'exagère? Il faut considérer la dimension historique.

RINK ATTENDANT:
>   Quelle dimension historique? Hey, il vient d'arriver
>   en ville?

DANDURAND:
>   Evidemment.

RINK ATTENDANT:
>   Eh bien, il faut lui montrer quelque chose
>   d'extraordinaire. Le Vieux Montréal. Le marché.
>   Le coeur du frère André.

DANDURAND:
>   Quand il est ton invité, tu lui montres le coeur du
>   frère André.

MORENZ:
>   You two are old friends, eh?

DANDURAND:
>   This nosey jerk? I'm gonna have him fired!

RINK ATTENDANT:
> That cock of the walk. Hey, you want to see the heart of Brother André?

MORENZ:
> You speak English!

RINK ATTENDANT:
> Is the Pope Catholic?

MORENZ:
> Ha, the Pope. Where you from?

RINK ATTENDANT:
> Listowel.

MORENZ:
> That's right near Stratford. What're you doing here?

RINK ATTENDANT:
> This is where they mustered me out. After the war.

MORENZ:
> And you never went back home? How come?

RINK ATTENDANT:
> What for?

> *He begins to exit.*

MORENZ:
> People talk . . . just like that.

DANDURAND:
> You'll pick it up. It's just a different language.

MORENZ:
> No, I mean . . . to each other.

> *DANDURAND leaves MORENZ momentarily.*

MORENZ returns to feeling "poetic" about the rivers.

They meet. Mingle. Join. Become one. A new force. Stronger than before. Different too.

He begins rehearsing again.

Excuse me, mademoiselle. You're very pretty. I know we haven't met, but this is Montreal. Where you say what you think and do what you say. And here's what I think . . .

He falters.

Uh, um . . .

DANDURAND: *overhearing him*
The best way is to be yourself.

MORENZ:
Oh, okay. What am I? . . . I'm a hockey player.

DANDURAND:
Alright.

MORENZ:
My name's Howie Morenz.

DANDURAND:
Good.

MORENZ:
I play for Stratford.

DANDURAND:
Oh.

MORENZ:
I'm the centre. All-star. Leading scorer. Most valuable player. Three years straight. How about a phosphate?

DANDURAND:

> Where will you tell her to meet you? The middle of
> the Ottawa River?

MORENZ:

> I'd really love to meet a French girl.

DANDURAND:

> Why?

MORENZ:

> They're so different.

DANDURAND:

> Different how?

MORENZ:

> I heard they really know about things. How to make
> things happen to you. That wouldn't happen at home.

DANDURAND:

> Howie, did you hear any other things about French-
> Canadians before you came here?

MORENZ:

> Like what?

DANDURAND:

> Like they're lazy or stupid or they all eat French
> fries and drink Pepsi-Cola.

MORENZ:

> Oh, yeah. Everybody knows that. I don't believe it
> though.

DANDURAND:

> Well, those things you heard about the French-
> Canadian girls . . .

MORENZ: *drooping*

> Yes? . . .

DANDURAND:
A lot of them are true.

MORENZ: *brightening*
They are?

DANDURAND:
But, Howie, you should be careful with the girls here.
It's very easy to hurt people. And for people to hurt
you. Especially when you don't understand them.
Do you know what I mean?

MORENZ: *pondering DANDURAND's remarks, then
brightening* Nope. Mr. Dandurand, if you were me,
what would you say to a French girl, a Montreal girl?

DANDURAND:
If I were you, I would say . . . Je suis un Canadien!

MORENZ:
I forgot about that.

He reaches for his cheque again.

*JOE MALONE enters, a great old player. He is
very depressed.*

DANDURAND:
Aha, the very man you should meet!

MORENZ:
Mr. Dandurand, I'm giving you this right now.

MALONE:
Just trying to skate off last night's game, Leo.

MORENZ:
You may not want to hear this.

DANDURAND:
Joe Malone, Howie Morenz.

MORENZ:

> Is he really Joe Malone? He looks like Joe Malone.
> Are you sure? He scored seven goals in one game.
> Forty-four in a season. That'll never be broken. This
> is a really big honour, Mr. Malone. I've followed you
> since I could skate.

MALONE:

> Nice to meet you, Howie. Some nicer time, we can
> talk.

> *MALONE exits.*

MORENZ:

> What happened yesterday?

DANDURAND:

> He was on the ice for the losing goal. Thinks it was
> his fault. Wasn't really, but . . .

MORENZ:

> That's just how I get! Once I could've scored, but my
> stick broke. I cried all night.

DANDURAND:

> Let's look at the dressing room . . .

MORENZ:

> Mr. Dandurand, stop! I have something for you. I'm
> returning it to you. My bonus cheque.

DANDURAND: *facing the music*
> You want to stay in Ontario.

MORENZ:

> Yes.

DANDURAND:

> You like it there.

MORENZ:
>It's super.

DANDURAND:
>Why?

MORENZ:
>Because . . . back home, I know exactly what life holds for me.

DANDURAND:
>Hmmm?

MORENZ: *faltering*
>I know just how I'm going to be until I die.

DANDURAND:
>Ah.

MORENZ: *panicking*
>There are no surprises!

DANDURAND:
>Uh-huh.

MORENZ:
>Is that French?

DANDURAND:
>What?

MORENZ:
>What you're doing.

DANDURAND:
>I'm not doing anything.

MORENZ:
>Yes, you are, you old fox!

He is surprised at himself.

Shit, I'm starting to act French already.

He chuckles.

DANDURAND: *laughing with him*
Take a chance. Feel at home.

> *He exits, leaving MORENZ behind, alone on the ice. MORENZ tries to feel at home there.*
>
> *VEZINA, who has been watching MORENZ since his arrival, alternately encouraged and then discouraged, throws the sticktorch to MORENZ. MORENZ catches it and carries on the tradition.*
>
> *The message board reads: "The Fastest Man Alive." The Canadiens are playing the Montreal Maroons, successors to the Wanderers. A French sportswriter is about to become the first Canadiens' SPORTSCASTER.*

SPORTSCASTER: *from the broadcast booth*
I don't care. I don't want to do it. Let somebody else in the pressbox do it. Why? There's no future in it. I don't care if the English are doing it. What? It's on? I'm on the radio? So what? Nobody's listening. Okay, I'll pretend. Good evening, fans of the Canadiens, if any of you are out there. I am about to describe a hockey game to you and you'll have to try to make sense of it with good use of your imagination. Good luck!

FIRST MAROON DEFENCEMAN:
There's no way he gets by us.

SECOND MAROON DEFENCEMAN:
He'd have to be three guys.

FIRST MAROON DEFENCEMAN:
>He goes left, I cut him down.

SECOND MAROON DEFENCEMAN:
>He goes right, I spread him on the boards like peanut
>butter.

FIRST MAROON DEFENCEMAN:
>Up the middle . . .

FIRST AND SECOND MAROON DEFENCEMEN: *together*
>We got a Morenz sandwich.

FIRST MAROON DEFENCEMAN:
>See him coming yet?

SECOND MAROON DEFENCEMAN:
>Nah, he probably quit. Oh, something's starting down
>there.

>*Whoost! MORENZ flashes through them like a
>streak.*

SPORTSCASTER:
>Oh, oh, oh! That was something special. I mean . . .
>and here comes Morenz up the ice towards the
>Maroons defence. He's almost there, and he cuts
>right through! Whew, fantastic! Oh my God,
>incredible!

>*The MOTHER enters. She is in her SON's
>bedroom.*

MOTHER:
>Jacques, Jacques, what are you doing up there? Get
>down! What radio? Howie qui? Oh, no, the bastards
>have invaded the bedroom!

>*Meanwhile, back on the ice . . .*

MAROON BACKCHECKING FORWARD:
It's okay, I got 'im. Good thing I backcheck. It's not
the glamour job, but somebody's gotta do it. Maybe
it's 'cause Mom always said the other kids were pretty
or smart, but I was so "responsible." I'm there when
there's hard slugging to do, and right now I'm gonna
cut in on Morenz and . . . Surprise! I'm back here
with you, Howie!

*Zip! MORENZ cuts right by him. The MAROON
BACKCHECKING FORWARD is the one who's
surprised.*

SPORTSCASTER:
Look! Look! What do you think of that? I mean,
here comes Morenz again . . . and he goes around the
Englishman like he's standing still in the mud!

MOTHER:
Quel pauvre pays, when its youth think about a
hockey team instead of the needs of their people.
What do you mean *our* team? How can *we* have a
hockey team?

Back on the ice . . .

MAROON GOALIE:
Alright, you frog-loving pansy. Let it fly. I'm up.
I'm ready. And I got the angle. You went too wide.
This net is covered like my granny's quilt. Blast it,
why don't you . . .

*The shot comes in, a swift wrist shot that lodges
in his glove without his even seeing it.*

. . . already! You don't score in the papers. You do
it on the ice. Hey, where you going?

MORENZ whizzes in behind the net.

MAROON GOALIE:
>Where's the bloody puck? Omygawd, I got it. I stopped Morenz! Hey, Sneaky.

>*He passes the puck to a MAROON RUSHING FORWARD who is lurking at the blueline.*

SPORTSCASTER:
>Morenz shoots! Oooooh, what a lucky save by the Englishman!

MAROON GOALIE:
>I stopped 'im.

MOTHER:
>You mean like we have a church? Like we have a language of our own? Ha! Howie, is that the name of a hero of our people? The name of an Anglais? I give up on you!

>*Back at the game . . .*

MAROON RUSHING FORWARD:
>I don't care if they think I'm a primadonna because I lurk around the blueline instead of backchecking like a terrier and digging like a gopher and working like a beaver, because when a break comes, I'm ready! Somebody's gotta be a glory hound. And here it is. And here I go. Everybody who's so "responsible" about their position caught up-ice behind me. I'm a streak from our blueline to their goal. Boy, do I love to score.

MOTHER: *relenting*
>It's not your fault. Come on now. Look, I'll make you a trade. Like they do in hockey. You get in bed and go to sleep. And I'll . . . give you the whole story of the game tomorrow morning on a little piece of paper by your bed. I'll go upstairs and listen. That's how.

MAROON RUSHING FORWARD: *panting*
> Whew, I wish they'd invent the redline. But no one
> can catch me now. Twinkletoes from Stratford's
> still behind our goal. There goes the blueline. That
> really stimulates me. I can smell the net. That little
> red light's gonna shine.

MOTHER:
> Yes, goals, assists, everything. The three stars too.
> Whatever they are. Now go to sleep. And God help
> Québec!

MAROON RUSHING FORWARD:
> Little headfake for their goalie, since I always throw
> in a move for lovers of the sport, and I bang 'er . . .

> *Whoost! MORENZ cuts in front of him and
> takes the puck off his stick.*

SPORTSCASTER:
> Look, look, Morenz stole the puck. I mean, he steals
> the puck right out from under him.

MAROON RUSHING FORWARD:
> Hey, who swiped my puck? Who stole my goal?
> Thief! Hey!

> *Whoost! MORENZ whirls and zips by him
> again, going in the opposite direction.*

SPORTSCASTER:
> He turns and wheels at centre ice.

FIRST MAROON DEFENCEMAN:
> We're gonna be ready for him next time. Right?

SECOND MAROON DEFENCEMAN:
> Believe it!

> *Whoost! MORENZ gets by them.*

SPORTSCASTER:
>He fakes left! He cuts right! Look . . . I can do it!
>On the radio!

MAROON GOALIE:
>I got your number. I know your moves. And I hate
>to see that puck go in the net!

SPORTSCASTER:
>He shoots . . .

MAROON GOALIE:
>Come on.

>>*Whoost! MORENZ shoots. The puck goes in the
>>net.*

SPORTSCASTER:
>. . . he scores!

>>*The red light goes on. The FANS are cheering.
>>The MAROON GOALIE is still set, waiting.*

MOTHER: *trying to get the language right*
>Howie Morenz, pour les Canadiens. Unassisted.

>>*MORENZ and the MAROONS exit.*

>>*The time clock reads 19:35. The message board
>>reads: "Regina: Two Strikers Killed in March of
>>Unemployed. Toronto: Conn Smythe Builds
>>Maple Leaf Gardens. Montreal: Maroons vs.
>>Canadiens."*

>>*The scene changes to a line at the ticket window
>>outside the Montreal Forum. The MOTHER
>>from the previous scene is standing there. An
>>English FAN enters.*

MOTHER:
>Est-ce que c'est la ligne pour les Canadiens?

ENGLISH FAN:
>Right. The game. Yeah. For the Maroons.

MOTHER:
>*Contre* les Canadiens?

ENGLISH FAN:
>Maroons won last night.

MOTHER:
>Les Canadiens aussi.

ENGLISH FAN:
>Good.

MOTHER:
>For you too.

ENGLISH FAN:
>Y'know, I can't really afford this game.

MOTHER:
>Me too. I do it for my boy. He's . . . y'know . . .
>il est fou des Canadiens.

ENGLISH FAN:
>Like me. I don't really get it. Kids can be sick.
>Foreman pushing hell out of me. Before I was laid
>off. Now I'm looking.

MOTHER:
>Yeah?

ENGLISH FAN:
>You looking too?

MOTHER:
>Me? French. Woman. I don't even try.

ENGLISH FAN:
>But the team goes well. I fly.

MOTHER:
> Huh.

ENGLISH FAN:
> Like nothing else matters.

MOTHER:
> Yes.

ENGLISH FAN:
> You too?

MOTHER:
> My son.

ENGLISH FAN:
> But maybe you too . . .

MOTHER:
> Me? From hockey? No way.

ENGLISH FAN:
> Maybe there's something wrong with my values. But, lookit, I can't do it myself. My life . . . I'm like every guy. No goal. No cause.

MOTHER:
> Uh-huh.

ENGLISH FAN
> Every day. Going to work.

MOTHER: *correcting him*
> Looking for work.

ENGLISH FAN:
> Right. Norma and the kids. They don't expect me to skate through the door at night and score a goal.

MOTHER:
> They don't cheer when you come in?

ENGLISH FAN:
>Yeah.

MOTHER:
>He's got a goal. A cause.

ENGLISH FAN:
>Who?

MOTHER:
>Howie.

ENGLISH FAN:
>Listen, I even root for him. Too bad he doesn't play
>for the Maroons.

MOTHER:
>Howie?

ENGLISH FAN:
>Being English.

MOTHER:
>Howie's French.

ENGLISH FAN:
>Morenz?

MOTHER:
>From Switzerland.

ENGLISH FAN:
>Come on.

MOTHER:
>They got French and Germans there.

ENGLISH FAN:
>Well, Morenz isn't French.

MOTHER:
>If they got both, there's a choice.

ENGLISH FAN:
>Look, we got French and English here, but if it's
>Duplessis, you got no choice.

MOTHER:
>Comme tous les Anglais. Faut tout posséder. Like
>always, the English. Gotta own everything.

>*She turns away.*

ENGLISH FAN:
>Oh, Morenz . . . Mor*awnz* . . . could be, I guess. Look,
>I don't care if he's a fuckin' Brit. Nobody on the
>Maroons lifts me like he does . . . and you got him.
>Remember how he beat Shore and Brimsek last year?

MOTHER: *relenting reciprocally*
>Those are two great English players . . .

ENGLISH FAN:
>I hope he never slows down. Days like these, you
>need a guy like that.

TICKET SELLER:
>No more greys or standing room for Saturday night.
>Lots of reds and blues still left.

MOTHER:
>Qu'est-ce que vous dites?

TICKET SELLER:
>Pas de gris ou de "standing room" pour le samedi.
>Y a des rouges et des bleux.

MOTHER: *to the ENGLISH FAN*
>Have a good time.

>*She leaves the line.*

80

ENGLISH FAN: *to the MOTHER*
>See you next game.

>*Turning to the TICKET SELLER.*

You too, maybe.

>*He leaves too, without buying a ticket.*

>*The time clock reads 19:37. The message board reads: "The Worst Is Over, Good Times Are Coming — P.M. Promises."*

>*MORENZ re-enters, streaking down the ice.*

SPORTSCASTER: *from the broadcast booth*
>Morenz picks the puck up behind his net. He crosses in front of the goal. Fast as ever. Well, almost. He streaks up the boards. Past a check. Past another. He wheels up the centre of the ice. Over the redline. Here comes Siebert. Morenz fakes left. He swings right. He's past Siebert. No, Siebert catches him with the tip of his hip. Morenz goes up in the air. He lands on his back. He's sliding down the ice. . . .

>*The whine of a long slide down the ice is heard.*

Here come the end boards. . . .

>*A crash is heard, then a crunch of bones that can be heard throughout the entire Forum. MORENZ's inert body is carried to centre ice.*

ENGLISH FAN:
>He'll be back. I'm telling you, he'll be back no matter how bad they say it is. And faster than ever. That bugger doesn't know how to slow down.

>*The ENGLISH FAN exits.*

SPORTSCASTER:

> The doctors say there are complications along with
> the original injury. He'll have to stay in the hospital
> a while longer. But it's not serious. They're just not
> sure he'll play again.

MOTHER:

> They traded him. You know what that means? He
> went away to another team. Chicago or something.
> No, we can't go see him when Chicago plays here.
> Because he won't be with them. He won't, that's
> all. Never! Forget about Howie.

> *The MOTHER exits.*

> *An English REPORTER is knocking on the back
> door of the Forum.*

ENGLISH REPORTER:

> Hey, lemme in. Come in. Thanks, Louie. I know I'm
> not supposed to come in this way, but the front was
> jammed. I'll just cut through the boiler room. Hope
> I'm not late. What a story! Jesus, what am I saying,
> a story? That's disgusting. I just hope they didn't
> bury him yet. Holy Mary, what a tragedy! What a
> story! Hey, where is everybody? Quiet as a tomb
> under here. I knew it couldn't be true. You don't
> hold a funeral at centre ice in a hockey rink. Even
> the Americans wouldn't do that. Even for Morenz.
> They must be in some church. . . .

> *He enters the arena. It is full — and silent.
> MORENZ's body lies at centre ice.*

> Oh my God! Every goddamn seat! In the whole
> fucking Forum!

> *The time clock reads 19:38.*

> *An English and a French BUSINESSMAN enter.*

ENGLISH BUSINESSMAN:

> One thing nobody's giving up is booze. Beer is bigger than ever. I need a new brewery and you can build it for me.

FRENCH BUSINESSMAN:

> That's very generous of you.

DANDURAND enters, down and out.

DANDURAND:

> Somebody want to buy a hockey team?

ENGLISH BUSINESSMAN:

> Now that's no investment. You want to look for something that fills people's needs and has a growth potential.

DANDURAND:

> Les Canadiens.

FRENCH BUSINESSMAN:

> Les Canadiens? Les Canadiens de Montréal?

DANDURAND:

> Oui.

FRENCH BUSINESSMAN:

> Cent cinquante mille.

DANDURAND:

> Cent cinquante mille? Pour les Canadiens? Vendu!

The message board reads: "$150,000.00."

The time clock reads 19:39. The message board reads: "Two-Piece Suits: $12.98. Everything Must Go! Our Loss, Your Gain!"

A French SPORTSCASTER is in the broadcast booth.

FRENCH SPORTSCASTER:

> Bonsoir mesdames et messieurs, ici la voix des
> Canadiens avec la joute de ce soir contre Toronto.
> Et voici les joueurs qui débuteront dans le match
> pour les Canadiens, et s'il vous plaît, excusez ma
> prononciation.

> *An English SPORTSCASTER enters, the
> REPORTER from the funeral scene. He shoves
> the French SPORTSCASTER over.*

ENGLISH SPORTSCASTER:

> 'Scuse me, Louie. Gotta make room for the new kid.
> Hello, hockey fans, you are about to hear the first
> live broadcast ever of the home games of the
> Montreal Canadiens.

FRENCH SPORTSCASTER:

> Ahem. *Ahem!*

ENGLISH SPORTSCASTER: *unperturbed*

> We'd especially like to welcome the old fans of the
> late lamented Maroons, among whom, me, the old
> rinkrat, counts himself. It was sad to see our
> favourites fold, but . . . we've still got the Canadiens,
> no matter how we felt about those Pepsi puck-
> carriers in the past. As the man might have said,
> "They're the only game in town."

> *The "new" Canadiens enter. They look like
> a pathetic and inept lot.*

> Anyway, you'd be surprised how many of the old
> Maroons have moved over to this team. I'd like to
> run down the line-up just to make you feel more
> at home, but . . . play is already underway. It's
> McNamara of the Canadiens in the corner. Passes
> it out to Lamarche . . .

> *He pronounces his name "Lamarch."*

. . . who misses, but Heffernan of the Habs grabs it
and passes to Toe Blake. Good old Toe!

FRENCH SPORTSCASTER: *trying to reclaim his territory*
Et maintenant, pour les Canadiens, c'est . . .

> *He pronounces the following name with
> difficulty.*

. . . Wat-son qui essaie un relai.

ENGLISH SPORTSCASTER:
Watson.

FRENCH SPORTSCASTER:
What?

ENGLISH SPORTSCASTER:
Watson, buddy.

> *Speaking into the mike.*

*Wat*son.

FRENCH SPORTSCASTER:
Wat-son à McNamara. A Heffernan, qui passe à . . .

> *With joy at being able to pronounce a French
> name at last.*

. . . Labrosse!

ENGLISH SPORTSCASTER:
Labrosse gets tangled up in his own skates, but
Langley gets him out of trouble.

> *These are bad days for Les Canadiens. They play
> terribly and, to boot, lose that distinctive free-
> wheeling style that used to characterize them.*

Ooooooh, McCormack rocks the Leaf forward! His teammates congratulate him. Whoops, the Leafs score.

FRENCH SPORTSCASTER:
Les Canadiens seem to care about nothing but maiming the opposition. But . . . here comes Fermier! He's all alone in the clear. Pass it! He's waiting! Help! Help! Au secours . . .

ENGLISH SPORTSCASTER:
And the Leafs snap it behind Bovier again. When will they put good old Bill Durnan in the net?

FRENCH SPORTSCASTER:
Une série de déflections héroïques par Bovier, mais les Leafs ont scoré. Y tombe sur la glace, c'est McMahon.

He mispronounces "McMahon."

ENGLISH SPORTSCASTER:
That's McMahon.

FRENCH SPORTSCASTER:
C'est écrit McMahon.

ENGLISH SPORTSCASTER:
That's English, not Eskimo! Broadcast white, for Chrissake!

FRENCH SPORTSCASTER:
Oh, there's a penalty to McCormack of the Canadiens.

ENGLISH SPORTSCASTER:
So the Habs will be shorthanded while McCormack sits out . . . Penalty? There's no penalty!

FRENCH SPORTSCASTER:
Oooooh, another penalty! To Heffernan!

ENGLISH SPORTSCASTER:
> That's baloney, Louie. Heffernan takes a wicked shot.
> He missed the net. But he hit the linesman!

FRENCH SPORTSCASTER:
> Carson is injured. Rivers has been ejected. O'Connor
> lost his stick. McCaffrey has been traded. And here
> come the *real* Canadiens, playing their classic game
> of speed and passing.

ENGLISH SPORTSCASTER:
> It's a rock 'em, sock 'em battle. The Habs are
> slaughtering the Leafs! Ooooh, Gag-non just got
> creamed! Those Frenchies should stay on the bench
> when real men battle.

FRENCH SPORTSCASTER:
> It's Gagnon to Mondou. A beautiful pass. Mondou
> to Majeau, an exquisite replay.

ENGLISH SPORTSCASTER:
> The Habs mass on their blueline.

FRENCH SPORTSCASTER:
> Les Canadiens roar forward.

ENGLISH SPORTSCASTER:
> It's the rough, tough Canadiens.

FRENCH SPORTSCASTER:
> It's the graceful, elegant Canadiens.

ENGLISH SPORTSCASTER:
> It's Burke.

FRENCH SPORTSCASTER:
> It's Lesieur.

ENGLISH SPORTSCASTER:
> It's Carson.

FRENCH SPORTSCASTER:
It's Gagnon.

ENGLISH SPORTSCASTER: *pronouncing it "Bow-cher"*
It's Boucher.

FRENCH SPORTSCASTER:
C'est Boucher.

ENGLISH SPORTSCASTER:
Bow-cher.

FRENCH SPORTSCASTER:
Boucher.

ENGLISH SPORTSCASTER:
It's a hit!

FRENCH SPORTSCASTER:
It's a pass!

ENGLISH SPORTSCASTER:
It's a fight!

FRENCH SPORTSCASTER:
It's a shot!

> *They fade in an interminable bilingual,*
> *bicultural wrangle that seems destined to*
> *go on forever.*
>
> *The MOTHER and her SON enter. Again,*
> *they are and are not the same as before.*

SON:
T'sais qui gagne?

MOTHER:
Eux autres. C'est même pas fini. Huit à un.

SON:

    T'sais qui a compté?

MOTHER:

    O'Connor, sur une passe de Getliffe et Watson.

SON: *having trouble with the names*

    O'Connor, puis Getliffe, Watson?

MOTHER: *bitterly*

    It's not like the good old days.

SON:

    J'ai une offre à jouer à Trois-Rivières.

MOTHER:

    Une autre?

SON:

    J'y pense.

MOTHER:

    Toi-là, tu restes, puis tu finis tes études.

SON:

    Pourquoi c'est faire? Les mathématiques? L'anglais?

MOTHER:

    You still want to play hockey for le club de hockey
    Canadien, you'd better learn English, my son.

SON:

    Arrête-moi ça.

MOTHER: *upset with him*

    It's like any job in Québec!

SON: *trying his English out on her*

    You mad at me?

MOTHER: *softening*
Non.

SON:
At the team?

He's found her out.

You've become a Canadien!

MOTHER:
No!

She is unconvincing.

Anyway, hockey, what's it matter? If they start their war, there's no hockey for you. They'll want you in their army.

This is a thought she's been afraid to broach.

Won't they?

SON: *answering her unasked question*
Well, I'll go.

MOTHER: *fearful and angry*
You'll go in the Army?

SON:
Yes. I'll fight to defend the country. But I won't go overseas. I'm not gonna fight for England!

The time clock reads 19:43. The message board reads: "Conscription If Necessary, But Not Necessarily Conscription."

The MOTHER and her SON exit.

A large, boisterous CROWD is pouring into the Forum for a game. The English FAN re-enters

with the CROWD. They take their places in the
stands.

ENGLISH FAN:
Sure, I root for 'em now. Even if they've had a few
bad seasons.

A VOICE FROM THE CROWD:
Anybody got a place to stay for an enlisted man and
his bride?

ENGLISH FAN:
They're not really French anymore. And anyway,
times change, thank God, if you know what I mean.

CROWD:
Victory Bonds! Anyone who doesn't buy is a traitor.

ENGLISH FAN:
I mean, a few years ago, I didn't even know if I'd be
around these days.

CROWD:
Take the King's shilling! Sign up for overseas!

ENGLISH FAN:
Now we're all up to our necks in this thing together.
Hell, the Canadiens are Montreal now.

The MOTHER re-enters.

CROWD:
The Army wants you too, lady.

ENGLISH FAN:
I think of them as the Montreal Canadians.

He sees that she is the same woman as before.

Hey, how are you now?

CROWD:
>Who wants to buy sandwiches, soft drinks, pop,
>coffee, playing cards, French safes, candy, hairpins,
>nail files, stamps, hankies, comic books . . .

ENGLISH FAN: *to the MOTHER*
>Come to see "our" team go at it, eh?

>*She snubs him.*

>Some of the Frenchmen maybe resent us . . .

CROWD:
>Jam for Britain! Fill the quota!

ENGLISH FAN:
>. . . for horning in on "their" team. I can see that.
>It's good to be loyal to your team. But there's bigger
>loyalties now . . .

CROWD:
>German sub sinks!

ENGLISH FAN:
>. . . and we've all got to do more than our share.

A VENDOR:
>Buy a souvenir programme for the boys overseas?

ENGLISH FAN:
>Sure.

THE VENDOR:
>Lady?

ENGLISH FAN:
>I'll buy one for the lady.

>*She ignores him.*

Everybody's working. Nobody's starving. They may be dying, but at least they're dying for something.

CROWD:
Got twelve dozen rubber spatulas. Wanta buy?

ENGLISH FAN:
We've got a cause and we're in it together.

CROWD:
Where's that kid's uniform?

CROWD:
Maybe he's got a wooden leg.

ENGLISH FAN:
We're all Canadians and nothing's so important these days as national unity, whether *they* want it or not.

ANNOUNCER: *from the broadcast booth*
Ladies and gentlemen, our national anthem. Mesdames et messieurs, notre hymne nationale.

The English FAN rises. The MOTHER does not. The ORGANIST begins to play.

ENGLISH FAN: *singing along with the organ music*
God save our gracious King,
Long live our noble King . . .

He is singing alone. The music stops.

ANNOUNCER: *repeating himself*
Ladies and gentlemen, our national anthem. Mesdames et messieurs, notre hymne nationale.

The MOTHER rises reluctantly. When the music starts, she sings, but she sings different lyrics than the English FAN.

MOTHER:
>A bas la conscription,
>A bas la conscription,
>La conscription . . .

>*The two versions of the song battle for*
>*precedence. Neither side seems able to prevail*
>*against the other, when the ROCKET skates on.*

ROCKET: *bringing the song to a halt*
Fuck this garbage! Play hockey!

>*The stick-torch is passed to him.*

>*The message board reads: "Enemy Has Rocket*
>*That Can't be Stopped."*

>*The Leafs enter. They circle the ROCKET*
>*warily as he moves toward the goal.*

Don't talk. Show me your moves. We'll see who's the
best. I volunteered for your war. They turned me
down because my bones break. That season I scored
fifty goals. I'm not fragile. I'm reckless. I'm not
"accident prone." I'm obsessed. My bones aren't
brittle. I don't care if they break. Except you can't
score in a cast. I don't think. I won't slow down.
Maybe I'll keep my head up, but I won't slow down.
Don't tell me about your great players from "over
there." Bring 'em home. I'll be here. Don't talk. Show
me what you care about. I'll show you what I care
about. We'll see. If I don't score, I'll burst. Do you
care like that? "That's what happened to Rocket the
night he didn't score. Exploded! Sweater splattered
on the first ten rows."

>*He is closing in on the Leaf goal.*

When I get close, it starts. Here, in my stomach. When
I cross the blueline. The net pulls me. When I can't
see it, I sense it. I can't sense it, I believe in it. Push

me back, it pulls me more. Like a cord that tightens the more you stretch. Top of the circle. My stomach gets worse. It wants to get out. It has to get out. It's a taste in my mouth. Hack me. Pile on me like I'm a table in the bargain basement: "Groan." I like it. I gotta. I'm gonna . . .

LEAF GOALIE:
Stop him!

ROCKET:
Pound me!

A LEAF:
He's a truck.

ROCKET:
Shove me!

A SECOND LEAF:
He's a Samson.

ROCKET:
Slash me!

A THIRD LEAF:
You're gonna kill yourself.

ROCKET:
Hammer me!

A FOURTH LEAF:
He doesn't care!

> The ROCKET is on top of the Leaf GOALIE.

ROCKET:
Hello!

LEAF GOALIE:
What're you gonna do now?

ROCKET:
> I don't know!

LEAF GOALIE:
> Then how can I know?

ROCKET:
> That's my secret. I got no strategy!

> *He turns his back to the Leaf GOALIE. The*
> *entire Leaf TEAM piles on top of him.*

LEAF GOALIE:
> Where you going now?

ROCKET:
> I'm going to score!

LEAF GOALIE:
> Cripple him!

FIRST LEAF:
> You cripple him!

LEAF GOALIE:
> Bring him down!

SECOND LEAF:
> He doesn't care!

LEAF GOALIE:
> What's he doing?

> *With his back to the net and moving away, the*
> *ROCKET flips the puck back and into the net.*
> *The shot ignites the red light. The bell rings.*
> *The CROWD erupts. The Leafs slide off the*
> *ROCKET's back like sweat. Released, he sags.*
> *The Leafs exit.*

> *The MOTHER enters, thoroughly drawn into*

the mystique of the team. She has finally
become a Canadien. As she sings the praises
of the TEAM, they gather around the ROCKET,
their "centre."

MOTHER:
Dieux du Forum,
Forum Gods!
Oh you, gloire à toi, Maurice.
Oh Rocket, aux pieds longs,
Tu es le centre de la passion
Qui régénère notre nation,
And you showed us the way and a light and a life.
Oh you,
Nous vous aimons et admirons!
And yet Maurice, you are the one,
Rocket, tu es le plus grand,
Parce que tu es le centre et le centre est Québécois,
Because you're the centre, and the centre is Québécois,
Parce que tu es le centre, et le centre est Québécois!

> *The TEAM is now marching to the song,*
> *"The Conquering Canadiens," as they proceed*
> *triumphantly through the NHL cities, defeating*
> *all comers.*

TEAM:
Nous irons dans le sud faire éclater nos couleurs,
Oui, nous reviendrons vainqueurs.
Like an army on ice, we march south every winter,
We return in the spring the conquerors!

> *In turn, they devastate all their opponents.*

Boston!
Chicago!
Detroit!
New York!

And, most fiercely . . .

Toronto!

> *On the word, "Toronto," the ROCKET scores his 500th goal and the TEAM celebrates deliriously.*

> *The scene changes to the dressing room after the game.*

> *The time clock reads 19:54. The English-Canadian BUSINESSMAN, who earlier denigrated a hockey team as "no investment," enters. He is identifiable in some way or other with a well-known Canadian beer.*

BUSINESSMAN:
> I can help you guys. I'll take you over for a million and a half.

> *The TEAM roars with laughter.*

A PLAYER:
> Where's that greasy kid stuff?

BUSINESSMAN:
> I'll put you on a sound basis. Two million?

> *They laugh again.*

A SECOND PLAYER:
> Drinks are on Butch!

BUSINESSMAN:
> You're good at what you do. So am I. Two and a half?

> *Further hilarity.*

A THIRD PLAYER:
> Who had Lindsay on the last goal?

BUSINESSMAN:
> I like being around you guys. Three million?

Louder than ever before . . .

A FOURTH PLAYER:
> How's your love life, Boomer?

BUSINESSMAN:
> My sales are down, but with you guys on the label . . .
> Three and a half. That's it!

They laugh him to scorn.

> Four million?

They are silent.

> You're bigger than beer!

TEAM:
> Sold!!!

The BUSINESSMAN exits.

The message board reads: "$4,000,000.00!!!!!"

The TEAM returns to its victory march.

Tour à tour trébucheront,
One by one they fall to us,
Like an army on ice, we march south every winter,
We return in the spring the conquerors!

Harvey, Moore, Geoffrion, et Maurice, Ti-Plante et
    l'grand Béliveau,
Pourraient gagner sans bâtons,
Pourraient gagner sans bâtons,
We return the conquerors,
Pourraient gagner sans bâtons!

The time clock reads 19:55. The message board reads: "Mange d' la merde."

The ROCKET and a LEAF fly into the corner after the puck. They fight for it. A REFEREE separates them.

REFEREE: *blowing his whistle*
Face-off!

LEAF:
Fucking frog!

The ROCKET attacks him.

Hey, what're you hitting me for?

ROCKET:
I'm gonna make hamburger out of you!

REFEREE:
Back off, Richard! Back off or it's a major . . .

The ROCKET backs off.

LEAF: *unbelieving*
Fuckin' frog!

The ROCKET attacks him again and throws him halfway across the ice.

REFEREE:
Hey, what's with you? Back off!

LEAF:
See that! He's a fruitcake!

ROCKET:
You heard it. You heard what he said.

REFEREE:

> That? You can't hit him for that.

ROCKET:

> You say!

REFEREE:

> Nobody reacts to that stuff.

LEAF:

> Not even your own people. Fuckin' animal!

REFEREE:

> We'd never finish a period if guys reacted to the little stuff.

LEAF:

> Look, I agree. There are times you gotta fight.

ROCKET:

> Like when?

LEAF:

> Everybody knows. Except you!

ROCKET:

> Tell me when!

LEAF:

> Geez, look . . .

> > *The LEAF and the REFEREE enact a confrontation between two players.*

> Your sister reeks from garlic.

REFEREE: *unfazed*

> Your father stinks from cabbage.

LEAF:

> Least I know where my father is.

REFEREE:
    Yeah? That's because he's in Kingston Pen.

LEAF:
    You spaghetti-eater!

REFEREE:
    Carp-eater!

LEAF:
    Cake-eater!

REFEREE:
    Mick!

LEAF:
    Spic!

REFEREE:
    Wop!

LEAF:
    Dago!

REFEREE:
    You're mother's a hooker!

LEAF:
    Your wife's in bed with a vibrator!

REFEREE:
    Fruit!

LEAF:
    Fairy!

REFEREE:
    Faggot!

LEAF:
    Queer!

He gooses the REFEREE.

REFEREE: *moving towards the LEAF*
I'll separate your skull . . .

> *They freeze before the blows land and turn to the ROCKET.*

LEAF:
Not for a name.

REFEREE:
Maybe for a really bad one. Nah, I can't even think of one.

LEAF:
Neither can I.

ROCKET:
Not for what he said?

LEAF:
No. Call me it. Go on. Can't you say it? Aw . . .

> *Speaking to the REFEREE.*

Fuckin' frog!

REFEREE: *to the LEAF*
Fuckin' frog!

> *To the other PLAYERS.*

Fuckin' frog!

> *To the ROCKET.*

Fuckin' . . .

> *The ROCKET throws down his gloves in a fury. The REFEREE hastily blows his whistle.*

REFEREE:
>Face-off!

>*The TEAMS line up.*

LEAF:
>You gotta get your values straight. Sometimes I think you're playing a different game from the rest of us.

>>*The REFEREE drops the puck. The ROCKET roars into the LEAF, then into all the other PLAYERS, then into the REFEREE. He devastates the rink. In the end, he is alone, victorious, swinging his stick.*

>>*CLARENCE CAMPBELL enters, the President of the National Hockey League.*

>>*The message board reads: "Clarence Campbell, Soldier, Scholar, Businessman, President of the N.H.L."*

CAMPBELL:
>It's happened again. Why? An "incident" on the ice. Why? I have investigated. Have you anything to add? I cannot allow my officials to be assaulted. You can appreciate that. I don't care whether your acts are merely the product of an unstable character or a deliberate defiance of authority.

ROCKET:
>I was defending myself.

CAMPBELL:
>Very effectively. I have nothing against you. Or any French-Canadian player. Or any player. But it isn't just you. It's the effect you have. On your teammates, your opponents. The fans. In Montreal and everywhere else. I've never seen anything like it in war or peace.

ROCKET:
> That's hockey.

CAMPBELL:
> The way *you* play it. Hockey is also a business, you
> . . . and I . . . are employees. It is inconceivable for a
> business to operate in this fashion. Can you imagine
> what would happen in a factory or office?

ROCKET:
> What do you want?

CAMPBELL:
> What I want doesn't matter. It is a question of what
> is the only honourable and . . .

ROCKET:
> "Sporting" thing to do?

CAMPBELL:
> Yes.

ROCKET:
> You want a public apology. Like the last time.

CAMPBELL:
> No. The time for tolerance and clemency is past.
> We both care about this game of hockey, don't we?
> Don't we?

ROCKET:
> Yes.

CAMPBELL:
> Well, the interests of hockey are bigger than one
> player . . .

ROCKET:
> Or six owners!

CAMPBELL:
>... who will not allow their merchandise to be
>maimed and broken!

>*He backs off.*

>At ease, Richard. Tell me, Richard, what is it that
>you want?

ROCKET:
>What I want?

CAMPBELL:
>Yes. Truly. What do you want?

ROCKET:
>To score goals.

CAMPBELL:
>That's not all there is to it, by God!

>*The ROCKET shrugs.*

>Please ... What do you want?

ROCKET:
>To win.

CAMPBELL:
>Not merely to play?

ROCKET:
>You gotta play to win.

CAMPBELL:
>This game has given you fame, wealth ...

ROCKET:
>Yes.

CAMPBELL:

> Well, where is your gratitude? You see, if you showed
> more, you might "win" more.

ROCKET:

> I don't understand you.

CAMPBELL:

> Two different languages.

ROCKET: *disagreeing*
> Like a war.

CAMPBELL: *retreating into formality*
> You're suspended for the rest of the season, including
> the playoffs. Most probably this means that you will
> lose the scoring championship, your most coveted
> goal, now within your grasp. In addition, your team
> will probably lose the pennant and the Stanley Cup
> as well.

> *The ROCKET starts to go. He is seething.*

> What are you going to do?

ROCKET:

> Me? Nothing.

> *The scene changes to the Forum.*

> *The time clock reads 19:55.*

> *The CROWD is restive. The ROCKET is not on
> the ice. He has been suspended. He sits with the
> CROWD in the stands.*

> *CAMPBELL arrives. He is taunting the CROWD
> by coming to the game after announcing the
> Rocket's suspension. The CROWD greets him
> with jeers and anger.*

109

CROWD:
>A bas, Campbell!
>Vive Richard!
>Did you sleep well last night, Campbell?
>Cochon anglais!

>*A tear gas cannister explodes in the Forum.*

>Lacrymogènes!
>Tear gas!

>*The CROWD coughs.*

>*The message board reads: "Tear Gas Explodes in Forum."*

>*The game is cancelled and victory forfeited.*

>*The scene changes to the street. The CROWD comes out of the stands and into the street.*

>Dans la rue!
>Lemme out of here!

>*The message board reads: "Crowd Pours Into St. Catherine Street."*

>*The Forum is dark.*

>*The CROWD is at first delighted to be in sole possession of the street. A kind of street festival begins. Chanting and singing is heard.*

>Québécois dans la rue, Québécois dans la rue . . .

>*The mood turns violent. A brick is flung through a store window. Oher bricks follow. The anger against Campbell is extended into anger against the English storekeepers along St. Catherine Street.*

The message board reads: "Store Windows Broken."

POLICE arrive. Sirens are heard. There is scuffling.

The message board reads: "48 Arrested."

The sound of riot begins to extend through the years following. It is as though the Richard-Campbell riot was only the opening shot of the Quiet Revolution and all that came after it.

The time clock and the message board record the subsequent events, while the sounds of riot, protest and street fighting continue:

19:62: "Thousands Protest in Front of CNR Headquarters."

19:64: "Bombs in the Streets of Westmount."

19:65: "Protest Against the Queen Crushed by Police."

19:67: "Huge Crowd Cheers 'Vive Le Québec Libre'."

19:68: "Beatings, Arrests in Anti-Trudeau Riot."

1969: "Riot Act Read in St. Leonard."

1970: "War Measures Act Proclaimed."

The ARMY has moved in. The streets are quiet at last. The Forum is dark and closed. The ice is empty. The lights fade.

Act Two
The Day of the Game

Act Two takes place during a single day. The message board reads: "November 15, 1976."

In this act, the time clock functions to give the time of day, not the year. It is 10:30 a.m.

JEAN BELIVEAU, the former Canadiens' great, is on the ice dressed in a business suit. He is alone. He has skates and has a hockey stick. The Forum is empty.

BELIVEAU:

It was the dream of every youngster in Quebec, Les Canadiens. I listened to Maurice Richard score his fiftieth goal in 1944. Over the radio. You know that thing about passing the torch? It was like that. I've got my office up there, but I like to come down here sometimes in the day. To skate. I keep my skates in the office. People who come to discuss maybe a booking or a promotion like to see them on the floor in there. Maybe it helps them believe I'm really the same Beliveau who was the hockey player. It was the Brothers of the Sacred Heart in Victoriaville who

taught me to play. They used to block shots with
their skirts. They spread their legs and caught the
puck. It used to get me mad. If I had stayed in
Victoriaville, I guess I would have worked for the
Hydro. My father worked for them. I worked for
them in the summer. Putting up lines, things like that.
I was taking courses in being an electrician, carpentry,
things like that. Then I went to Quebec City. I was
like a god there. I was eighteen, nineteen years old.
They gave me cars. I was making more money than
my father and I was just eighteen, nineteen years old.
When you're a star, there's always somebody not
happy. If I only scored one goal, somebody would
say, "Jean, what was wrong last night?" So I was very
quiet. Very calm. They treated me like a god. I had
to figure out a way to behave. People saw I was quiet
and they could think what they wanted about me.
Inside I felt things and people knew that. In Quebec,
I started to take an interest in community things.
Opening stores. Community centres. Ice-cream
stands. Things that people knew about. I'm well-
known for my work in the community. Tomorrow
I have to go to the new Eaton's in Senneville. I have
a little contract with RCA. Promotional stuff. Next
day is the United Appeal kick-off banquet. And I
have a little something with a coffee maker. Super
Coffee Maker. I do a thing on TV for them. . . .
I wouldn't want to be a coach. I work with the
community, go out and speak to groups. I've done
that all my career. Mr. Pollock has the responsibility
to make the decisions about the team and the players.
Of course I take part. Tonight, for example, I have
to decide whether to flash on the results during the
game. But I'm really best-known for my work in the
community. Running the hockey operation, making
the decisions about the team. that's another area.

He is slightly out of breath.

I've slowed down a bit. Maybe I should go to the
W.H.A.

A shift now, with a sense of assurance.

I was a centreman, so the main thing was Making the Play. You had to decide so many things all the time. If you're coming down and the defenceman makes a move on you, you have to calculate whether there's enough room left for you between him and the boards for you to get through. And also, if you will be too deep to Make the Play. That depends on whether your wingmen are coming back, how fast they're moving in, whether the forwards of the other team are backchecking . . . Of course, it's based on your instincts, your reactions. But no . . . you do have to think about it. You have to consider it and make a decision, even though it's very fast. Of course, it's all in relation to how quickly you skate. If you're moving very fast, you have to take all the factors into account very quickly. If you skate slower, you have more time to mull the situation over, but you have fewer options. But then, as I said, I only have limited experience in decision making. You can see I'm not really the executive type.

He exits.

The time clock reads 11:00 a.m.

DAVE KIRK, an all-star forward for the Canadiens, enters on his way to the Forum.

KIRK:

The best thing in the world is to be a Montreal Canadien on the day of a game. When you become a Canadien, you become part of something big and old. You're a part of Montreal . . . No, Montreal is a part of you. People recognize you . . . not just as an athlete.

People have been noticing him as he makes his way to the Forum. Finally, he arrives there.

The Forum. The cathedral of hockey. Walking into it when you're on the team, it's like being the Pope in Rome . . . No, it's better. It's . . . being a Canadien.

He enters the Forum. Two GUARDS, one English and one French, are at the door arguing over a newspaper.

ENGLISH GUARD:
Stop worrying, you'll be dead and buried before it happens. Me too.

FRENCH GUARD:
Look . . . statistics, figures. They can write it on your grave.

ENGLISH GUARD:
You dumb Pepsi. You believe it because it's in the paper. In *that* paper?

KIRK is there, but they don't notice him.

FRENCH GUARD:
Aw, it's even in the *Montreal Star*.

ENGLISH GUARD:
What about the weather? You believe the weather forecast too?

KIRK:
Hi, Jake. Hi, Jacques.

FRENCH GUARD:
Hiya, Davey.

ENGLISH GUARD:
I remember when they said inflation was over. You remember that?

KIRK starts to move away.

But this one is really impossible. It's like Toronto winning the Cup. Oh, hi, Dave. Sorry, I didn't notice you. My kid asked me to ask you . . .

He brings out a piece of paper and goes after KIRK for his autograph.

KIRK returns to the entrance.

Well, it's for the grandson really. Now one for the granddaughter so she won't get jealous.

CLAUDE MOUTON enters, the Forum announcer and a compulsive bilingualist.

MOUTON:
Bonjour, les gars. Hello, boys.

KIRK:
What time have you got, Claude?

MOUTON:
Il est onze heurs et quart. Time, eleven-fifteen. Très grande soirée ce soir. Big night tonight. A bientôt. See you soon. Au revoir. Too-de-loo.

He exits.

KIRK:
I gotta be at the language class.

ENGLISH GUARD:
Yeah, just this one for the little niece.

Speaking to the French GUARD.

I been hearing this stuff since the fifties. Every four years, they panic. Everybody jumps up and down and worries.

FRENCH GUARD:
>The English businessmen say they're gonna run away to Toronto.

ENGLISH GUARD:
>And it always turns out the same.

FRENCH GUARD:
>Yeah, but one of these times . . . Surprise! Then, what happens to us? They close the Forum. Move the team somewhere else.

ENGLISH GUARD:
>Thanks, Davey. Nice guy, eh? Reading it over and over won't make it true. Relax.

FRENCH GUARD:
>We bet?

ENGLISH GUARD:
>Like it's a game? You bet.

FRENCH GUARD:
>Okay, I feel better.

>*HARRY, one of the team managers, enters. He pounces on KIRK.*

HARRY:
>Hiya, Davey. How's my all-star?

KIRK:
>Hi, Harry.

HARRY:
>Glad I caught you, kid. Just step over here. I'll help you off with the jacket.

KIRK:
>I can take it off myself. Hey, what's it for?

HARRY:
>Get measured.

KIRK:
>Measured for what?

HARRY:
>Your blazer.

KIRK:
>What blazer?

HARRY:
>For the handbook. Don't worry.

KIRK:
>What handbook? I gotta be somewhere.

HARRY: *indicating a door*
>Yeah, just go in here for a minute.

KIRK:
>What's in here?

HARRY:
>Radio. Commercial for charity. They'll tell you what
>to say.

KIRK: *going in the direction in which HARRY has pointed
him* I don't have to be told what to say.

>*He goes in and comes back out.*

HARRY:
>What?

KIRK:
>It's the French.

HARRY:
>Oh. Must be in here.

He points him to another door.

KIRK goes in there and comes back out.

Now what?

KIRK:
I'm too tall.

HARRY:
Huh? C'mon over here.

KIRK: *following him*
Harry, I gotta be somewhere.

HARRY:
Yeah, but this is important. You're a big star.

KIRK:
If I'm a big star, why do you treat me like a kid?

HARRY:
Kid? Ha! What a kidder!

KIRK:
Harry, I'm an adult.

HARRY:
Sure you are, kid.

KIRK:
And I've got an important appointment. So give me
my jacket.

HARRY:
Right away after.

KIRK:
No. I'm not going to be treated like a child.

HARRY:
Okay, so what do you want?

KIRK:
I want my jacket!

HARRY:
Soon as you tape the bit.

KIRK:
I'm not going another step till I get it! Understand?

HARRY:
Awww, poor baby.

> *KIRK grabs his jacket and starts to move away.*

Hey!

KIRK:
What?

HARRY:
What d'you think it is to be a star on the Canadiens anyway?

> *HARRY exits.*

> *The time clock reads 11:30 a.m.*

> *Three ANGLOPHONE CANADIENS are waiting for their French lesson to begin.*

FIRST ANGLOPHONE CANADIEN: *holding up a pen*
Qu'est-ce que c'est?

SECOND ANGLOPHONE CANADIEN:
C'est une plume.

FIRST ANGLOPHONE CANADIEN:
Non, c'est un stylo.

THIRD ANGLOPHONE CANADIEN:
> What's the difference? He doesn't know what to do with it anyway.

SECOND ANGLOPHONE CANADIEN:
> "X" on the contract. He learned that and then he quit school.

FIRST ANGLOPHONE CANADIEN:
> Yeah? I'm really gonna impress her today.

> *KIRK arrives ready for his French lesson.*

> Hey, Dave. Take the Pepsi challenge. How do you say hockey stick?

KIRK:
> Bâton de hockey.

SECOND ANGLOPHONE CANADIEN:
> Hey, hey, he's been studying.

THIRD ANGLOPHONE CANADIEN:
> Brown-noser!

SECOND ANGLOPHONE CANADIEN:
> Did you bring an apple for teacher?

FIRST ANGLOPHONE CANADIEN:
> A "pomme."

THIRD ANGLOPHONE CANADIEN:
> Oh-ho, this man's gonna run for Prime Minister. "I promise to hold the country together in both languages."

SECOND ANGLOPHONE CANADIEN:
> Oh, here she comes . . .

FIRST ANGLOPHONE CANADIEN:
> It's not her.

122

THIRD ANGLOPHONE CANADIEN:
How can you tell? All those French teachers look
the same.

*The two GUARDS stop the French TEACHER
who has tried to enter.*

ENGLISH GUARD:
Mademoiselle . . .

*They indicate that she has to sign the book. She
signs and starts to move towards the class. The
STUDENTS rise.*

STUDENTS:
Bonjour, mademoiselle.

TEACHER:
Bonjour, la classe. Asseyez-vous. Comme vous
pouvez voir, je ne suis pas votre professeur régulier.
Aujourd'hui nous ne suivons pas la routine.

*The STUDENTS look blank. The TEACHER
tries again.*

Ce n'est pas une journée ordinaire. C'est une journée
*extra*ordinaire. Extraordinaire! Mademoiselle
Chapleau, votre professeur régulier . . . Mademoiselle
Chapleau? L'autre professeur?

THIRD ANGLOPHONE CANADIEN:
The other one.

TEACHER:
Oui. Mademoiselle Chapleau est allée faire son devoir.

Still, they are blank.

Est allée faire son devoir? Hummm?

She mimes "she has gone to vote."

TEACHER:
Le morceau de papier. Le petit "eeks." Plier le papier.
Et dans la boîte.

The STUDENTS are still blank.

Hummm?

She mimes a huge ballot.

L'Union Nationale . . .

She turns thumbs down to them.

Les Libéraux . . .

She puts them right at the bottom.

Et le Parti Québécois!

She raises a triumphant fist.

THIRD ANGLOPHONE CANADIEN:
Voting! The other one went to vote!

The TEACHER sighs.

TEACHER:
Oui, monsieur. Elle est allée faire son devoir. Je suis
Mademoiselle Miron. Miron.

STUDENTS:
Mademoiselle Miron.

TEACHER:
Eh bien, messieurs. C'est une drôle de place pour une
classe de français. Une drôle de place? . . .

She gives up explaining that.

Enfin, j'ai enseigné un peu partout. Voyons. Votre dernière classe était . . .

She checks the register and is shocked.

. . . il y a trois semaines! C'est une assez longue absence pour des gens à un niveau si primitif! Et avant ça, encore deux semaines! Laissez-moi vous dire messieurs, si vous ne pouvez pas venir en classe dans une manière plus régulière, je ne peux pas voir comment vous allez pouvoir maîtriser la belle langue de Molière!

FIRST ANGLOPHONE CANADIEN:
Excuse me, Miss Miron, but we have a special problem with regular attendance.

TEACHER:
Excusez-moi, monsieur, mais quand nous sommes en classe, je regrette de ne pas pouvoir comprendre un seul mot de ce que vous dites. Pas un mot. Notre première règle: le français seulement. Mais si vous voulez nous expliquer en français quelle est la nature de votre problème, ça serait utile à tous et à toute.

FIRST ANGLOPHONE CANADIEN:
Okay, d'accord. Nous travaillons dans Montréal.

TEACHER: *already impatient with the low level of his knowledge of French* Oui, monsieur, allez-y!

FIRST ANGLOPHONE CANADIEN:
Et aussi nous travaillons, uh . . . outside de Montréal.

TEACHER:
Uh, uh, uh . . .

FIRST ANGLOPHONE CANADIEN:
Pas dans Montréal?

To the other ANGLOPHONE CANADIENS.

What's "outside?"

KIRK:
  Dehors.

FIRST ANGLOPHONE CANADIEN:
  Dehors de Montréal!

TEACHER:
  Tout le monde.

STUDENTS:
  Dehors, dehors, dehors.

TEACHER:
  Et alors?

THIRD ANGLOPHONE CANADIEN:
  I'll try. Nous allons toujours . . . No, "toujours" is
  wrong. What's the other one?

FIRST ANGLOPHONE CANADIEN:
  Souvent.

THIRD ANGLOPHONE CANADIEN:
  Right. Souvent. A une autre place. A des autres
  places.

  *He sits down, quite satisfied with this minor
  effort.*

TEACHER:
  Mes pauvres étudiants. Si c'est trop difficile pour vous
  de m'expliquer pourquoi vous ne pouvez pas venir
  en classe d'une manière plus régulière, vous pouvez
  peut-être m'expliquer pourquoi vous voulez apprendre
  le français de toute façon. Eh?

126

She mocks their accents.

Pourquoi-voulez-vous-apprendre-le-français? Vous, monsieur?

> *She points to the SECOND ANGLOPHONE CANADIEN, by far the least promising linguist of the STUDENTS. The other ANGLOPHONE CANADIENS grimace as he rises.*

SECOND ANGLOPHONE CANADIEN:
Il y a des garçons . . . des autres garçons . . . avec nous . . .

TEACHER:
Garçons?

KIRK: *to the SECOND ANGLOPHONE CANADIEN*
"Garçons" are little boys.

SECOND ANGLOPHONE CANDIEN: *embarrassed*
Stuff it, Dave. You're so smart. What d'you know? Boys are boys.

THIRD ANGLOPHONE CANADIEN:
Awright, awright, I'll do it. Nous travaillons avec des gars qui parlent anglais à nous. Et nous voulons parler français à . . . à . . . à . . . to them!

TEACHER:
Ah-ah-ah, monsieur. En français. Qu'est-ce que c'est? A . . . à . . .

> *She gets them all trying for the word.*

STUDENTS:
A . . .

TEACHER:
A . . .

STUDENTS:
    A...

TEACHER:
    A...

STUDENTS:
    A...

TEACHER: *with enormous frustration*
    A eux!

STUDENTS:
    A eux!

> *The TEACHER is furious. She lapses into English.*

TEACHER:
    You never come to class! You never learn anything
    when you are here! And on top of that, the people
    you work with speak English to you anyway. So I'm
    saying to you .... Oublier! Forget it! C'est pas la
    peine! It's not worth the trouble!

FIRST ANGLOPHONE CANADIEN:
    No...

SECOND ANGLOPHONE CANADIEN:
    Hell, no...

THIRD ANGLOPHONE CANADIEN:
    We're not gonna quit. Not us.

TEACHER:
    Mais qui êtes-vous donc? Des freaks du bilinguisme?

SECOND ANGLOPHONE CANADIEN:
    Shit! I didn't come here to get insulted.

FIRST ANGLOPHONE CANADIEN:
> We're trying, eh? The other guys don't even come.

THIRD ANGLOPHONE CANADIEN:
> Christ, we always have fun with the other teacher.

> *They sulk.*

> *The TEACHER starts to pack up.*

TEACHER:
> Okay. Il faut vouloir apprendre le français. *We* don't care if you learn French.

KIRK:
> Listen, Miss Miron. The basis of this club has always been teamwork. French guys, English guys, they always got along for the sake of the team.

TEACHER:
> Monsieur, comme je vous ai dit, je ne comprends pas un seul mot de ce que vous dites.

SECOND ANGLOPHONE CANADIEN:
> Oh, forget it, Dave. What're you bothering for? You want to be insulted?

KIRK:
> It's a tradition. It's a legend, the unity between the French and the English on the club.

TEACHER:
> Ah, la fameuse "unité nationale!"

KIRK:
> Except the language of it has always been English, no matter how many French guys there were. And that wasn't fair.

FIRST ANGLOPHONE CANADIEN:
> You're talking to a wall.

SECOND ANGLOPHONE CANADIEN:
> Un mur!

TEACHER:
> Très bien, monsieur!

KIRK:
> And we figured if the French guys learned enough
> English to understand us in the game, we ought to
> do as much for them!

TEACHER:
> Game! What game? Qui êtes-vous donc? Who are you?

FIRST ANGLOPHONE CANADIEN:
> You mean you don't know?

SECOND ANGLOPHONE CANADIEN:
> What do you think this place is . . . Disneyland?

TEACHER:
> Le Forum, mais . . .

THIRD ANGLOPHONE CANADIEN:
> Les Canadiens. We are les Canadiens.

FIRST ANGLOPHONE CANADIEN:
> Right.

SECOND ANGLOPHONE CANADIEN:
> Yeah.

TEACHER:
> Les Canadiens? Le club de hockey, "les Canadiens?"
> I should have known!

KIRK:
> Why? Does that make a difference?

TEACHER:
> Well, a little. I remember the old days. When I was a little girl. Oh, the Rocket! And the great riot against the English, uh . . . businesses on Ste. Catherine!

FIRST ANGLOPHONE CANADIEN:
> Does that mean our class is back on?

TEACHER:
> Well, it's a special situation. We could try a different approach. Why don't we discuss your last road trip?

> *They frown at the thought.*

> Well then, I have another idea . . .

> *She teaches them a song.*

> Mes joueurs ont tous des beaux patins . . .

STUDENTS: *singing*
> Mes joueurs ont tous des beaux patins . . .

TEACHER:
> Des beaux patins . . .

STUDENTS:
> Des beaux patins . . .

TEACHER:
> Et pis skate, skate, skate . . .

STUDENTS:
> Et pis skate, skate, skate . . .

TEACHER:
> Patine plus vite . . .

STUDENTS:
> Patine plus vite . . .

TEACHER:

> Shoot, shoot, shoot, il faut bien lancer,
> Gotta shoot to score.
> Win, win, win, si tu veux gagner,
> Faut compter encore.

> > *They join in, taking verses in turn, building up
> > to a list of what the players eventually have, in
> > reverse order . . .*

ALL:

> Un gros paycheque!
> Un gros jockstrap!
> Des belles bretelles!
> Un chandail propre!
> Des beaux bas blancs!
> Des bonnes jambières!
> Des épaulettes!
> Des beaux patins!

> > *They all have a grand time singing and learning.
> > Bilingualism can indeed be fun, but does it really
> > solve anything? As they finish the song, KIRK
> > moves away from the other ANGLOPHONE
> > CANADIENS.*

FIRST ANGLOPHONE CANADIEN:

> Hey, Davey, what's with you? We're starting to get
> along fine now.

KIRK:

> Yeah, she doesn't like us when we're English, but she
> likes us fine when we're the Canadiens.

FIRST ANGLOPHONE CANADIEN:

> What's the matter with that? She likes us, doesn't she?

KIRK:

> She does, she doesn't . . .

FIRST ANGLOPHONE CANADIEN:
> Hey, come on. We *are* the Canadiens.

KIRK:
> Yeah, and what if she decides tomorrow she doesn't
> like the Canadiens? I dunno. It's not the way it used
> to be.

FIRST ANGLOPHONE CANADIEN:
> Hell, Davey, in the old days, nobody'd have even
> bothered to learn French.

KIRK:
> I know. They just rolled along.

> *The TEACHER and the ANGLOPHONE*
> *CANADIENS exit.*

> *The time clock reads 1:00 p.m.*

> *KIRK is wandering through the corridors of the*
> *Forum looking at the pictures on the walls of*
> *the great old teams and stars. He is chatting*
> *amiably with the portraits.*

Hiya, Newsy. Haven't seen you in a while. We been
on the road. 'Cause of the circus. Newsy, when you
played with a separated shoulder, or that time with a
concussion, it wasn't for the money. Not then. I
know that. It was something else that drove you,
was it . . .

> *He falters.*

Aw, keep in shape!

> *He moves on.*

Hi, Vezina. You're practically in your underwear
compared to goalies now. Lots of punishment, eh?
But you held them off. I know the old T.B. got you,

133

but . . . it was all worth it back then because . . .
because . . . Aw . . .

He mimes a quick wrist shot.

Beat ya!

He continues on.

Morenz! What a corney pose! Won't get any
commercials looking like that. Howie . . . did you
ever feel in your days . . . that people didn't . . .
just 'cause you were from . . . I mean . . . Nah.
'Course not . . . Now, Rocket, you were over here . . .
No, up here . . . Where'd you go?

*He spies LIONEL, an old Canadien player from
the great teams of the fifties. LIONEL is French.
His name is pronounced "Lee-o-*nel.*"*

Lionel!

LIONEL:
You remember me?

KIRK:
Sure. It was in the dressing room before the oldtimers'
game last season, right?

LIONEL:
You getting in shape for tonight?

KIRK:
Killing time. You know how it is the day of a game.
I should have my meal soon and then get some sleep.

LIONEL:
The pre-game nap. That was my favourite part of the
day of the game.

KIRK:

We've been working on our power play. Scotty's got some good drills.

LIONEL:

Those poor Leafs. They've got it tough enough already.

KIRK:

Yeah.We're playing well. But you guys were pretty good on the power play too.

LIONEL:

Yes. Of course, we never had any strategy. We never said, "You go here, I'll go there." "What the hell! Gimme the puck, I'll score."

KIRK:

Yeah. That's the best way.

LIONEL:

I'd just go into the corner and I'd throw out the puck. I figured he'd be there. And he was.

KIRK:

Him?

LIONEL:

Rocket.

KIRK:

Oh, sure. What're you doing now?

LIONEL:

Oh, old Canadiens never die. Just eat, drink, live high . . .

KIRK:

That's how it is, isn't it? Way up there . . .

LIONEL:

> 'Course, not like you guys these days, with the big
> bucks.

KIRK: *a little embarrassed*

> Well, it's not so different. Where you living then?

LIONEL:

> Lac St. Jean.

KIRK:

> Nice place to retire.

LIONEL:

> I work with kids there.

KIRK:

> Oh.

LIONEL:

> Make something of them. Teach them self-reliance.

KIRK:

> You mean like . . . grow their own food?

LIONEL:

> Hell, I mean kill it!

> *They laugh.*

> You like to hunt?

KIRK:

> Not really.

LIONEL:

> College guys.

KIRK:

> Just two years.

136

LIONEL:

Hey, we were dumb, eh? We got taken.

KIRK:

You mean the money?

LIONEL:

Hey, I don't blame you guys. It's great. Get what you can. Crisse, you play for twenty-five years, at the end you're not ready for anything else.

KIRK:

I guess it's just because of when the expansion happened.

LIONEL:

And you were there. What a way to make a living . . . playing the Colorado Rockies. I would've liked that.

KIRK:

Yeah, but you had some really great times in those days.

LIONEL:

You think so, eh?

KIRK:

Things were different then. More exciting.

LIONEL:

Are you kidding? The night train to Chicago? Leave at eleven Saturday, after the game. Get to Chicago at seven the next night. Game starting at eight. Whooo . . . now you got jets.

KIRK:

And jet lag!

LIONEL:

On my first road trip, I was so shy. I never was out of Québec before. The reporters said to Dick Irvin,

"Doesn't the kid speak English?" He said, "I don't even know if he speaks French!"

They laugh.

We stayed up all night, you know. Playing hearts. You still play?

KIRK:

Yeah, on the plane.

LIONEL:

But we never gambled. We didn't want winners and losers on the team. It's not like that now, is it?

KIRK:

Uh-uh.

LIONEL:

Crisse, guys play each other for the Stanley Cup and then they run a hockey school together in the summer.

KIRK: *thinking of the old days*
It sounds great.

LIONEL:

Yeah, that and fifty cents'll get you on the Métro.

KIRK:

But you guys . . . that team . . . You meant so much to people.

LIONEL:
You too.

KIRK:

Yeah, but so many other things matter today too. I dunno . . .

LIONEL:

> Y'know . . . Us . . . We were just hockey players.
> That's all we wanted to do. Play hockey. We never
> thought we . . . stood for something. Is that right?

KIRK:

> What?

LIONEL:

> Stood for?

KIRK:

> Yeah, stood for.

LIONEL:

> We just played. And what was great . . . that was
> what the people wanted from us. It was enough.
> Like nobody needed anything else. As long as we
> won. If we didn't win, I don't know what they
> would've done.

KIRK:

> Yeah.

LIONEL:

> But you guys, you came along in time for the real
> good times in hockey.

KIRK:

> Yeah, I guess.

> > *They have run out of things to say to each
> > other.*

LIONEL:

> I gotta go, Dave. Good luck tonight.

KIRK:

> You too.

LIONEL heads for the door. The two GUARDS are snoozing there.

LIONEL: *comfortable with the old Forum personnel*
Hey, regarde qui dort à la switch. Les deux souris aveugles.

FRENCH GUARD:
Oh-ho, le buffon de Chicoutimi.

LIONEL:
Hey, Lac St. Jean.

ENGLISH GUARD:
Who let you in? You made enough trouble when you were playing. Go on, get out there and vote. Did you vote yet?

FRENCH GUARD:
The last time he voted was for Dief the Chief. Then he gave up.

ENGLISH GUARD:
Remember when Duplessis was the Chief? He came to every game to see the Rocket.

FRENCH GUARD:
One Maurice came to cheer for the other Maurice. Vas-y, Maurice! Vas-y, Maurice!

ENGLISH GUARD:
Now they only come when they think they'll be on the TV.

KIRK: *calling after him*
Lionel . . .

LIONEL:
Yes?

KIRK:
> Happy hunting.

LIONEL:
> Good dreams to you.

> *LIONEL exits.*

> *The time clock reads 3:30 p.m.*

> *KIRK is taking a nap, but it turns into a nightmare — the nightmare of an English speaking Canadian in Quebec. He is in goal.*

KIRK:
> Okay, guys. We're the Canadiens. Les Canadiens. And tonight is going to be the biggest test we've ever had. Hey, what'm I doing in here? I'm a winger. Where's Ken Dryden? You gotta be crazy to play goal. Everybody shoots at you.

> *His TEAMMATES are gathered around him, somewhat ghoulishly.*

> I'm gonna really need everyone to help out. No matter what the rest of them do, no matter what the rest of the world does, we stick together 'cause we're a unit, we're a team, we're a unit, we're a team . . .

TEAM:
> Uni-team, uni-team, uni-team, uni-team . . .

KIRK:
> Stick together. Don't leave me alone.

> *His TEAMMATES hear a whistle blow.*

TEAM:
> Aieeeee . . .

*They go streaming away from him, screaming
wildly.*

KIRK:

Guys, wait! Don't leave me alone. They'll sneak up,
you poor crazed bastards . . .

*An English and a French SPORTSCASTER
are in the broadcast booth.*

ENGLISH SPORTSCASTER: *from the broadcast booth*
Behind the brilliant puck stopping of Ken Dryden . . .

KIRK:

Hey, no, it's me!

ENGLISH SPORTSCASTER:

. . . the Canadiens are continuing their imperious
march into hockey history!

FRENCH SPORTSCASTER: *from the broadcast booth*
Despite inconsistent goaltending, the *tricolore* are
holding their own on the ice.

ENGLISH SPORTSCASTER:

But the opposition is forming in the other end of
the rink!

FRENCH SPORTSCASTER:

They are readying a challenge for the overrated
netminder!

ENGLISH SPORTSCASTER:

He's a lonely, heroic figure . . .

KIRK:

Not by myself!

FRENCH SPORTSCASTER:

It's getting closer!

ENGLISH SPORTSCASTER:
Bearing in on him!

FRENCH SPORTSCASTER:
A menacing force!

KIRK:
You . . .

ENGLISH SPORTSCASTER:
The famous television celebrity and talk show host . . .

FRENCH SPORTSCASTER:
And candidate for the people's party . . .

ENGLISH SPORTSCASTER:
Star of Quebec's most popular television programme . . .

> *LISE PAYETTE enters, sliding down the ice behind her talk show desk.*

LISE:
Appelez-moi Lise!

KIRK:
Help! Hey, guys . . .

LISE:
Appelez-moi Lise!

KIRK:
Help! Please . . .

LISE:
Appelez-moi Lise!

KIRK:
My team . . . where are you?

> *His TEAMMATES have turned into onlooking tormentors.*

LISE:

Appelez-moi Lise!

KIRK:

Au secours . . .

LISE:

Attention!

TEAM:

Attention!

KIRK pays attention.

LISE: *syrupy*
Appelez-moi Lise.

KIRK: *trying hard, but managing poorly*
Lise . . .

LISE:

Ahahahaha . . . NON! Lise . . .

KIRK:

Lise . . .

LISE:

Arrrrrgggggghhhhh . . .

KIRK:

Lise?

LISE:

Fini!

KIRK:

Please, I can do it. Let me try once more. L . . .
L . . . L . . . L . . .

His TEAMMATES mock his efforts.

LISE: *suddenly, in an upper class English accent, like the Queen* Really, my good chap, I do believe you people have no voice of your own. Not a jot . . .

TEAM: *also in an English accent*
You can't miss it. Indubitably. 'Ave a cup of tea. Cucumbers . . .

KIRK:
We do! We do have our own voice. It's just different.

LISE: *very American*
Well, I mean, it's pathetic, that's all. You got nothing to say. No wonder you're such losers!

TEAM: *also American*
Hey, man. Cool it, man. I don't go lookin' for trouble. Rock it, man . . .

KIRK:
It's not true!

LISE: *in an English accent*
You may call me Liza.

In an American accent.

Call me Liz. Appelez-moi Lise. Ecoutez, n'écrivez pas! Lise, Lise, Lise, Lise . . .

TEAM: *joining in with her*
Lise, Lise, Lise, Lise . . .

LISE exits.

KIRK:
Lise, you're a liar! We do have our own voice and we use it just as well as you.

The ORGANIST begins to play the "Hockey Night in Canada" theme.

145

ENGLISH AND FRENCH SPORTSCASTERS: *from the
broadcast booth*   And now, our between periods
interview guest . . .

Suddenly, KIRK is on television.

KIRK:
It's a pleasure to be here, Brian, and finally have a
chance to *speak* . . .

ENGLISH AND FRENCH SPORTSCASTERS:
Now, tell us, Dave . . .

KIRK:
Yes?

ENGLISH SPORTSCASTER:
Did you or did you not want to be a Maple Leaf as a
small child?

FRENCH SPORTSCASTER:
Are you now or have you ever been a member of a
team with orange sweaters?

ENGLISH SPORTSCASTER:
Why did you pass the puck to Larry Robinson?

FRENCH SPORTSCASTER:
Why did you refuse to pass the puck to Guy Lafleur?

ENGLISH SPORTSCASTER:
He didn't!

FRENCH SPORTSCASTER:
He did!

ENGLISH SPORTSCASTER:
What did Claude Ruel say to Scotty Bowman?

FRENCH SPORTSCASTER:
What did Scotty Bowman say to Claude Ruel?

ENGLISH SPORTSCASTER:
Why does a Canadien wear red suspenders?

FRENCH SPORTSCASTER:
Why did the Maple Leaf cross the blueline?

> *In the midst of this lunacy, KIRK hears a
> voice. It is SYLVIA TYSON singing the gentle,
> lyrical ballad, "Four Strong Winds." KIRK is
> drawn to her as she sings, "Think I'll go out to
> Alberta . . ."*

KIRK:
There it is. That's our voice. Close to nature. Quiet,
but really caring. Sort of innocent, but really sincere.
I knew we had it. Now sing to them about Ontario . . .
"There is a town in North Ontar-i-o . . ." It's so good
to hear you. For a minute I almost believed we didn't
have our own voice. It's so soft and hard to hear. But
the more you sing, the more I remember . . .

> *As SYLVIA TYSON SINGS, she turns into
> PAULINE JULIEN singing a rousing nationalist
> song of Québec in French.*

Hey, that's not the words. That's not the tune. Hey,
what're you doing? Who are you? Stop! Bring back . . .
you know . . . that other song . . . whatever it is . . .

> *PAULINE JULIEN pursues him singing.*
>
> *Suddenly, the English and French SPORTS-
> CASTERS are back.*

ENGLISH AND FRENCH SPORTSCASTERS: *from the
broadcast booth*   And now for the highlights of the
last three periods of Canadian history . . .

ENGLISH SPORTSCASTER:
The shut-out of the French Canadians at the Plains
of Abraham . . .

FRENCH SPORTSCASTER:
>The overtime victory by Dollard des Ormeaux . . .

ENGLISH SPORTSCASTER:
>The elimination of the Americans in the War of 1812 . . .

FRENCH SPORTSCASTER:
>The sparkling teamwork of the Patriotes of 1837 . . .

ENGLISH SPORTSCASTER:
>The power play of 1867 . . .

FRENCH SPORTSCASTER:
>The comeback of Louis Riel . . .

ENGLISH SPORTSCASTER:
>The CPR . . .

FRENCH SPORTSCASTER:
>The FLQ . . .

ENGLISH SPORTSCASTER:
>World War I . . .

FRENCH SPORTSCASTER:
>Henri Bourassa . . .

ENGLISH SPORTSCASTER:
>World War II . . .

FRENCH SPORTSCASTER:
>Maurice Duplessis . . .

ENGLISH SPORTSCASTER:
>Pierre Trudeau . . .

FRENCH SPORTSCASTER:
>A bas la conscription . . .

KIRK:
>Hey, what about hockey?

ENGLISH SPORTSCASTER:
>Can we see that on the replay?

KIRK:
>What happened to the Canadiens?

ENGLISH SPORTSCASTER:
>Where is the replay?

>>*The English and French SPORTSCASTERS exit.*

>>*KIRK is exhausted, depressed, alone. MADAME BENOIT enters.*

MADAME BENOIT:
>Now you come over here and sit down and I'll fix you a nice meal.

KIRK:
>Oh, Madame Benoît, thank God, it's you!

MADAME BENOIT:
>Of course. Because you know that although I'm one of *them*, I've always liked you.

KIRK:
>Yes, I know. You share your recipes with us.

MADAME BENOIT:
>I've always enjoyed cooking. And it doesn't matter who I cook for, because all over the world, the language of friendship between the peoples is . . . eating!

TEAM:
>Let's eat! Let's eat! Let's eat! Let's eat!

KIRK:

>I'm hungry too.

MADAME BENOIT:

>Well, I'm just going to mix up a few things and you
>will be amazed at the results!

KIRK:

>It smells so good. Nobody liked me . . . even though
>I was a Canadien . . .

MADAME BENOIT:

>That's all over now. Now I just add a touch of this.

>*She touches him.*

>A pinch of that.

>*She pinches him.*

>A good, big stir!

>*His TEAMMATES are stirring him.*

>It's almost ready now! And look who we're having
>for dinner!

>*His TEAMMATES are preparing to devour him.*
>*He searches desperately for help.*

KIRK:

>The fans. Our fans. My fans. My last hope. Tell me
>you're with me. Cheer me. Talk to me . . .

FANS: *from the stands*
>Get a job!

KIRK:

>What? I give up. I'm ready. No, I won't give up. I am
>what I am. Go on, shoot!

150

He is a goaltender in goal and a prisoner before a firing squad.

Go on, vote! Go on, shoot! Go on, vote! Go on, shoot! Go on, vote! . . .

The scene changes to the dressing room of the Montreal Canadiens.

The time clock reds 6:00 p.m.

The PLAYERS are getting ready for the game. Some PLAYERS are still arriving.

FIRST PLAYER: *an Anglophone*
So he says, "Go on, vote." I say, "Where!" I was looking for one of those booths. He says, "Right behind the cardboard." It came up to here.

He indicates chest high.

I felt like I should be taking a leak.

SECOND PLAYER: *a Francophone*
What's the matter? You never voted before?

FIRST PLAYER:
No.

SECOND PLAYER:
Why not?

FIRST PLAYER:
I wasn't old enough.

THIRD PLAYER: *an Anglophone, to KIRK who is waking up* Hey, Davey, wake up. What's going on? Have a dream?

KIRK:
I guess so.

THIRD PLAYER:
 What was it?

KIRK:
 I dunno. Something about voting. I can't remember.
 Couldn't have been very interesting.

 A FOURTH PLAYER enters, a Francophone.

FOURTH PLAYER:
 Salut, les gars. Oh, boy, it's good to get in here.
 Everybody out there in that city is crazy. Half of
 them are voting for the goddamn PQ.

FIRST PLAYER:
 Goddamn right.

FOURTH PLAYER:
 I couldn't believe it. Some of my own friends. My
 family!

FIRST PLAYER:
 Shit!

FOURTH PLAYER:
 My brother-in-law. I said to him, "This is the greatest
 country in the world. Look at us, we can go any-
 where . . . Vancouver, Toronto . . . and we feel at
 home." And he says, "I don't wanta feel at home in
 Vancouver and Toronto. I want to feel at home in
 Québec!"

FIRST PLAYER:
 Hey, listen, this guy explains to me why he's voting
 for the PQ . . .

THIRD PLAYER:
 He's a separatist. What else?

FIRST PLAYER:
 No, he's a federalist!

THIRD PLAYER:
And he's voting PQ?

FIRST PLAYER:
Yeah, he says, "Look, if the PQ makes a strong
showing, it'll scare the piss outa the Liberals and
they'll really get their act together and then they'll
be strong enough to hold off the PQ when the
crunch comes!"

THIRD PLAYER:
Jesus!

FOURTH PLAYER:
"Aren't you proud of your country?" he said. I said,
"Which country?" That stopped him, I thought.

SECOND PLAYER:
What'd he say?

FOURTH PLAYER:
He said, "You've got a problem, my friend." I said,
"Me?!!"

SECOND PLAYER:
You can't talk to some people.

FOURTH PLAYER:
"Anyway," I said, "I voted Union Nationale." They
were the separatists before René Lévesque was born!

THIRD PLAYER:
Hey, look, I don't know why some of you guys voted
U.N. You know they're not gonna win. You just
split the anti-PQ vote.

FOURTH PLAYER:
Well, we just knew some of the guys who were
running, y'know?

SECOND PLAYER: *referring to the FOURTH PLAYER*
And guess who thinks maybe *he's* gonna run for the
U.N. one of these days . . .

FIRST PLAYER:
Those separatists, they wouldn't know what to do
with the power. If the PQ gets in, you'll see grass in
St. Catherine Street in fifteen years!

THE OTHER PLAYERS:
Yeah. Right. Damn right.

FIRST PLAYER:
That's a good line, eh? I heard another guy say it . . .

FOURTH PLAYER:
Yeah, but there's "grass" in St. Catherine Street right
now . . .

They laugh.

THIRD PLAYER:
Look, Trudeau's a smart guy, right? He's not just
sitting back in Ottawa. Half his goddamn majority
comes from Quebec. You bet he's got his finger in it.

FIRST PLAYER:
I told this guy, "English and French can work
together and get things done." He says, "Gimme
one example of French and English working together
like that?" I says, "The Canadiens!"

THE OTHER PLAYERS:
Yeah, right . . .

SECOND PLAYER:
I would've said that.

FIRST PLAYER:
He says, "That's the only example in the history of
the country!"

154

THIRD PLAYER:
>That can't be true.

FIRST PLAYER:
>I couldn't think of another one.

>*This remark slows them all down.*

THIRD PLAYER:
>The Plouffe family!

FIRST PLAYER:
>The what?

THIRD PLAYER:
>Yeah, they used to do it in English one night and French the next.

SECOND PLAYER: *with a sexual innuendo*
>That sounds tremendous.

FIRST PLAYER:
>Well, we're solid on this team, eh? We're solid in here!

THE OTHER PLAYERS:
>Yeah, right . . .

>*They are starting to get hyped for the game.*

KIRK:
>How d'you think the Rocket voted?

SECOND PLAYER:
>Oh, the Rocket. He's pretty bitter, eh?

KIRK:
>He wouldn't vote separatist . . .

SECOND PLAYER:
>You never know what the Rocket is going to do.

FOURTH PLAYER:
Just like when he was going in on goal!

> *They laugh, the remark cracking the tension. The*
> *Rocket seems to be the only Canadien in doubt*
> *on the issue.*

> *HENRI RICHARD enters, the former Canadien*
> *great, younger brother of the Rocket. He has*
> *retired only a few years previous and is looking*
> *fit. He is a prosperous owner of an excellent*
> *tavern.*

KIRK:
Hi ya, Henry!

SECOND PLAYER:
Henri, comment ça va?

THIRD PLAYER:
Henry . . . I didn't know if you'd be here to watch
us tonight.

RICHARD:
What else is happening in Montréal today?

THIRD PLAYER:
I thought you might have a tennis date or something
important.

FIRST PLAYER:
Hey, Henry, that was a good article you wrote in the
paper telling people to vote Liberal.

RICHARD:
Oh, you're reading French now?

FIRST PLAYER:
Well, some guy told me about it.

SECOND PLAYER:

    Henri, c'est vrai qu' t'as écrit c' t'article-là?

RICHARD:

    Qui d'autre?

KIRK:

    Hey, Henry, what're people saying about the election over at the tavern?

RICHARD:

    Well, you know we can't serve until after the voting is finished.

KIRK:

    Oh, right.

RICHARD:

    But they come in anyway . . . to get an argument.

KIRK:

    Oh, yeah?

RICHARD:

    Lots of them . . . especially the young ones. They think I should be for the PQ.

THIRD PLAYER:

    Why?

RICHARD:

    Because of the troubles I had sometimes with the coaches.

THIRD PLAYER:

    So what?

RICHARD:

    They say, "What about the coaches? They were both English, right?" I say, "That's not politics, that's hockey. Y a pas de politique là-d'dans!"

THIRD PLAYER:
> What'd he say?

SECOND PLAYER:
> He says he likes your pretty blue eyes . . .

RICHARD:
> I tell them, "Look, this is the greatest country in the world to live in. It gives you the best chance to get what you want." Look at me. When I was a kid, a little kid in Québec, I had two dreams.

KIRK:
> What were they, Henry?

RICHARD:
> Well, one was . . . I dreamed I would be on the Canadiens.

THE OTHER PLAYERS:
> Hey, right . . .

FIRST PLAYER:
> The master of the face-off!

SECOND PLAYER:
> Our captain!

KIRK:
> What was the other dream?

RICHARD:
> I dreamed I would own a tavern.

> > *He says this with utter conviction and simplicity. It proves his point about the separatism debate.*
> >
> > *They give a cheer that contains a lot of relief.*

THIRD PLAYER:
> Hey, Scotty's on his way in.

RICHARD starts to leave before the coach arrives.

RICHARD:
You're all invited over to the taverne to watch the
results after the game.

KIRK:
You think they'll be in by then?

RICHARD:
Oh, yeah. We can celebrate.

KIRK:
Bye, Henry.

SECOND PLAYER:
Salut, Henri.

*RICHARD exits as the coach, SCOTTY
BOWMAN, starts to enter.*

FIRST PLAYER:
Awright, we're gonna drive these guys through the
bottom of the standings tonight!

THE OTHER PLAYERS:
Yeah, right . . . Get 'em . . .

BOWMAN enters the dressing room at this point.

FOURTH PLAYER: *to the FIRST PLAYER*
Nice timing, Peter.

SECOND PLAYER:
As usual.

They laugh.

*The time clock reads 7:30 p.m. It is time for the
pre-game pep talk. BOWMAN has the problem
of a coach who has a team that almost never*

loses. Throughout his speech, the PLAYERS are
silent. They pay virtually no attention to him.

BOWMAN:

I'm telling you, this is a big one tonight. You think
it's going to be easy? These guys've lost about
nineteen games in a row. They're really hungry.

He tries a variation.

They're forty-five points behind us in the standings
and that makes 'em mad! We gotta beat 'em down a
little more.

Trying a different tack.

They got nothing to look forward to. Beating us
could be the big thing in their season.

And another.

If we take these guys for granted, we lose our edge.
Then we meet the Bruins and the Flyers . . . Wham!
This could be the most important game of the season!
If you guys got anything on your minds tonight
except hockey, forget it! Look around you. See
what's written up there . . .

On the wall or on the message board is written:
"To You from Failing Hands We Throw the
Torch, Be Yours to Hold It High."

Those plaques. Those names. Those achievements.
Those guys on all those great teams never thought
about anything except winning the game. Nothing
else mattered. Nothing else still matters. That was
the Canadiens. That is the Canadiens. You're playing
on their ice and they're looking over your shoulder.
Don't bother looking back, 'cause they're right there
with you. Okay? Alright? Are you ready? Let's go . . .

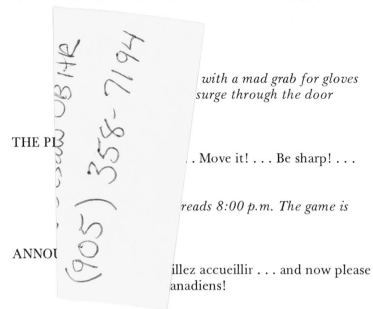

with a mad grab for gloves
surge through the door

THE Pl

. Move it! . . . Be sharp! . . .

reads 8:00 p.m. The game is

ANNOU

illez accueillir . . . and now please
anadiens!

The Canadiens enter as the ORGANIST plays
their theme song.

There is a silence from the CROWD.

Ahem. Veuillez accueiller . . . nos Canadiens!

There is still no response. The PLAYERS circle
uneasily on the ice.

SECOND PLAYER:
It's spooky.

FOURTH PLAYER:
It's nuts.

SECOND PLAYER:
Usually I can't hear anything 'cause there's so much
noise. Now I just can't hear anything.

KIRK:
It's like a funeral.

FIRST PLAYER:
It's like Toronto.

THIRD PLAYER:
Or Vancouver.

BOWMAN: *from the bench*
Is anybody here interested in a hockey game?
Halloooo up there . . .

AN ECHO:
Hallo, hallo, hallo . . .

The whistle sounds. The game is on.

THE PLAYERS:
Skate, skate . . .

KIRK:
On your wing . . .

BOWMAN:
Switch . . .

THIRD PLAYER:
I got centre . . .

*The puck goes into the corner. The PLAYERS
pile in after it and hold it for a face-off.*

SECOND PLAYER:
Cover 'im, Davey!

KIRK:
Freeze it! Freeze it!

*As they jam each other against the boards, the
message board comes alive. It reads: "Election
Results: Parti Québécois: 3. Liberals: 4."*

*The CROWD roars in reaction to the election
results.*

SECOND PLAYER: *hearing the CROWD's response*
> Ah, there they go.

KIRK:
> About time.

FIRST PLAYER:
> How come they're yelling now? We're not doing anything.

KIRK:
> I dunno.

THIRD PLAYER: *looking at the message board*
> Hey, lookit! What's that?

KIRK:
> Oh, no! They're showing the election results.

FOURTH PLAYER:
> This is a hockey game. How come they do that?

KIRK:
> I dunno. Don't ask me.

FOURTH PLAYER: *irritated*
> I am asking you . . .

KIRK: *irritated as well*
> *I'm* not paying any attention to it.

> > *The message board changes to: "Parti Québécois: 9. Liberals: 8."*

> > *The CROWD roars.*

SECOND PLAYER:
> Nothing to worry about.

KIRK:
> The PQ's are winning, aren't they?

FIRST PLAYER:
>Yeah, but it's just the results from Montreal. They come in first.

SECOND PLAYER:
>It always starts this way.

KIRK:
>It does?

FIRST PLAYER:
>They got all those radicals in Montreal.

KIRK:
>Ah, radicals.

SECOND PLAYER:
>Nothing to worry about.

KIRK:
>I'm not worried. Are you worried?

FIRST PLAYER:
>No. We just told you, kid. Nothing to worry about.

KIRK:
>Is anybody worried?

SECOND PLAYER:
>No, nobody's worried. Play hockey, for Chrissake!

>>*The message board changes to: "Parti Québécois: 13. Liberals: 10."*

>>*The CROWD roars again.*

>>*The action is in front of the Canadien net.*

GOALIE:
>Get it clear!

THIRD PLAYER:
> Knock 'im off it!

GOALIE:
> Up and out! Up and out!

THIRD PLAYER:
> Clear it! Hey!

GOALIE:
> Not in front! I can't see. Shit! I can't see . . .

> *A shot is coming in.*

KIRK:
> I got 'im.

> *He flings his body onto the ice in front of the shot and makes a brilliant block.*

GOALIE:
> Dave, that was brilliant!

KIRK: *looking up at the CROWD*
> Where's my cheer?

> *The CROWD is silent.*

GOALIE:
> *I* thought you were great!

KIRK:
> Thanks. That and fifty cents'll get me on the Métro.

> *The message board starts to change again. There is a buzz from the CROWD.*

> Shit, there they go again . . .

GOALIE: *watching the opposition*
> Outa my way! Here they come again!

KIRK: *watching the message board*
Here it comes . . .

> *The message board reads: "Parti Québécois: 22. Liberals: 16."*

> *KIRK is blocking the goalie.*

GOALIE:
Where is it? Who's got it?

> *There is a shot on goal.*

> *The GOALIE just manages to glove it.*

KIRK: *referring to the message board*
Pretty close.

GOALIE: *referring to the shot on goal*
You're not kidding!

> *Meanwhile, elsewhere on the ice.*

FIRST PLAYER:
Hey, listen to this. If it goes on this way, we're gonna have to take Dryden out and put Larocque in. Get it?

SECOND PLAYER:
That's not funny.

FIRST PLAYER:
How about this? From now on you can call me Jean-Pierre Mahovlich!

SECOND PLAYER:
C'mon, you. Play hockey!

FIRST PLAYER:
Hey, have you got your passport ready for the game in Toronto?

SECOND PLAYER:
> Shut up, I said. Cut it out!

> *Turning to the audience.*

> These old guys, they're scared. They worry about their investments and their restaurants and their player pensions because of the election. Not me. Me. I'm a young guy. All my life I only cared about one thing. Be a Canadien. Get on the ice in the Forum. Hear the cheers of the crowd in my ears . . .

> *The message board changes to: "Parti Québécois: 24. Liberals: 14."*

> *The CROWD roars again.*

> . . . Like that! Hey, I'm not doing anything. Why're you cheering now?

> *He sees the message board.*

> What d'you want, hockey or politics? You're fucking me up! You want politics, go to the Paul Sauvé Arena. You don't want hockey, get out of here. Go on, get out! Get out!

> *The message board changes to: "Parti Québécois: 34. Liberals: 15."*

> *The CROWD is in an uproar.*

> *The PLAYERS try to concentrate on the game, but they can't.*

FOURTH PLAYER:
> Screw the game! We gotta do something about this.

> *They forget about the game and all go out into the CROWD to argue with the fans.*

THE PLAYERS:

> Look, we're the Canadiens and you're our fans. You
> gotta trust us. We've been the vessel of Quebec's
> hopes for so long, the symbol of your aspirations.
> So we gotta know what we're talking about when it
> comes to what's best for the future of Quebec . . .
> And we're telling you, this separatism is wrong!
> Stick with federalism. Stick with Canada. It's a
> wonderful, beautiful country. You wouldn't want to
> lose British Columbia. We've been out there and we
> can tell you, it's fantastic! You'd miss it, even if
> you've never seen it. And federalism is profitable.
> It makes us part of a continent-wide economy.
> Without federalism, we'd be an economic backwater.
> Are you listening? Our living standards would
> plummet. But most of all, federalism is a beautiful
> idea. Do you hear that? It takes people out of their
> narrow, self-centred nationalism and forces them
> to expand their horizons and join hands with others.
> Get it? In this sense, Canadian federalism is a heroic
> experiment. The wave of the future with Canada in
> the lead. Right? As the Prime Minister said, "To
> throw away this noble vision of federalism in favour
> of narrow nationalism and separatism would be a
> sin against the spirit and humanity."

> *New election results are coming up on the*
> *message board.*

> *The CROWD begins to roar again.*

> Listen to what we're saying! It's for the good of all
> of us. Who could know better than the Canadiens
> what's good for Quebec? Listen, you screaming
> idiots. Pay attention!

> *The message board reads: "Parti Québécois: 48.*
> *Liberals: 20."*

> *The CROWD is near pandemonium.*

How can we be wrong about this? We are the spirit of Quebec, you stupid goats! We always have been! We're you! And we're telling you, you're full of shit! Goddammit, take the wax out of your ears!

They retreat back, away from the CROWD, to the ice and each other. As they go, they turn and call names at the CROWD.

Oafs! Stones! Stocks! Blindmen! Fools! Dolts! Clowns! Buffoons! Simpletons! Dullards! Toads! Donkeys! . . .

They are back together on the ice in a state of total frustration. The CROWD is in an ecstasy over the election results and ignores the team. The PLAYERS turn to each other.

Fuck this garbage! Play hockey!

They start to skate again.

Hey! Let's go! Skate! On your wing! Up and out! Take the man! Centre, centre! Skate, skate! Slot! Point! In! Shoot! Shoot! Shoot! Score! . . .

KIRK scores as the result of a magnificent team effort. It is a classic Canadien goal.

The Forum erupts. The Canadiens raise their sticks high and embrace each other. They chant: "Les Canadiens! Les Canadiens! Les Canadiens!"

They look up to see that the eruption from the CROWD has been for the final results of the election, not for their goal.

The message board reads: "Victoire Parti Québécois." The CROWD is chanting: "Victoire P.Q.! Victoire P.Q.!"

The Canadiens lower their sticks and look at them. They are no longer weapons handed down to them since 1759.

CROWD: *singing the following lines over and over*
A partir d'aujourd'hui, demain nous appartient,
Un pays aujourd'hui si vraiment on y tient. . . .

The Canadiens retreat from the ice. Only KIRK stays on.

The CROWD surges onto the ice and takes over. The ice turns into a battlefield once again where, this time, the French celebrate victory.

The time clock reads 11:00 p.m. The celebration has wound down.

KIRK is still standing on the ice. He is surrounded by a WOMAN and two QUEBECOIS.

THE WOMAN:
C'est un miracle!

FIRST QUEBECOIS:
C' pas vrai. Dis-moi que c' pas vrai.

SECOND QUEBECOIS:
Combien de sièges maintenant?

FIRST QUEBECOIS:
Soixante-huit!

THE WOMAN:
Hey, c'est fini dans Mercier.

FIRST QUEBECOIS:
T'sais qui a gagné?

THE WOMAN:
Godin. Bourassa yé chomeur!

SECOND QUEBECOIS:
>On a gagné tout! Tout le monde a gagné!

>*To KIRK.*

>*Gagné!*

KIRK: *with a stiff upper lip*
>Oui. Gagné. Quatre à deux dans le match.

FIRST QUEBECOIS:
>Oh, les Canadiens. We don't need them now.

SECOND QUEBECOIS:
>Soixante-huit à trente-trois!

KIRK: *bitterly*
>Yeah. You won.

FIRST QUEBECOIS:
>No, man. *We* won.

KIRK:
>Yeah.

FIRST QUEBECOIS:
>Hey, take it easy, man. Look, there's still electricity.
>I bet you the Métro is still running.

SECOND QUEBECOIS:
>Hey, hey, en français!

>*To the WOMAN.*

>Hey, viens-tu au Paul Sauvé avec nous autres?

FIRST QUEBECOIS: *to KIRK*
>Everybody's going to the Paul Sauvé Arena for the
>victory party. You can come too.

SECOND QUEBECOIS:
> Lévesque va faire un discours.

> *To KIRK.*

> Lévesque!

THE WOMAN: *regretfully*
> Non, ch' peux pas. J'ai pas de babysitter.

FIRST QUEBECOIS:
> On y va.

SECOND QUEBECOIS: *to the WOMAN*
> Salut Québécoise!

> *To KIRK.*

> Relax, man. Relax . . .

> *The two QUEBECOIS leave. KIRK is left alone with the WOMAN.*

KIRK:
> What're you gonna do now?

THE WOMAN:
> Us? We gotta go to work tomorrow.

KIRK:
> Yeah, but . . .

> *He indicates the election results.*

THE WOMAN:
> We don't know what's going to happen.

KIRK:
> Separatism?

THE WOMAN: *correcting his terminology and using the French pronunciation* Indépendance? Maybe.

KIRK:
Socialism? Revolution?

THE WOMAN:
Nobody knows that. Maybe.

KIRK:
Then what're you so excited for?

THE WOMAN:
We stood up.

She pauses, then decides to explain further.

For many years, we let others stand up for us. Like . . .

KIRK:
Les Canadiens?

The WOMAN nods.

THE WOMAN:
Now we do it ourselves.

KIRK: *understanding her explanation, even if it saddens him* Bonsoir.

THE WOMAN:
Good night.

She exits.

KIRK:
Being a Canadien *used* to be the greatest thing in the world. Before they stood up.

173

ANNOUNCER: *from the broadcast booth*
Dernière minute du jeu. Last minute of play.

The time clock reads 11:30 p.m.

KIRK is walking home alone. Under a street light, he comes upon a group of little KIDS playing street hockey with a ball and broadcasting their own plays, as kids will. He watches them play.

FIRST KID:
Lafleur is tearing down the wing. He flies into the corner. They jam at it. Lafleur still has it. It's glued to his stick. He's looking for Shutt . . .

He passes the ball over to another KID.

SECOND KID:
It comes out to Shutt. Shutt shoots! Shit!

THIRD KID:
He hit the post!

FIRST KID:
Don't feel bad, Shutt. We'll get you another shot.

THIRD KID:
Now Lemaire has it. He whirls at the blueline. He feeds it to Lafleur.

FIRST KID:
Lafleur passes neatly onto Shutt's stick.

SECOND KID:
Shutt winds up. He shoots . . . No! . . . He passes back to Lafleur.

FIRST KID:
Lafleur's got it. He shoots, he scores!

174

FIRST AND SECOND KID:
>Yayyyyy!

THIRD KID: *becoming a Russian player*
>But here come the Russians again.

>>*The FIRST and SECOND KID become Russians as well.*

FIRST KID:
>Aha! The Russians.

SECOND KID:
>The Russians are coming!

THIRD KID:
>Yakushev brings it up the right side. He fires a rink-wide pass to . . . Kharlamov!

SECOND KID:
>Kharlamov takes it and cuts in on goal.

>>*He drops a pass.*

FIRST KID:
>He leaves a drop pass for Maltsev. Maltsev fires a wicked drive!

FOURTH KID: *playing the goalie*
>Dryden stops him for the Canadiens!

THIRD KID:
>It's loose in front of the net. Yakushev bangs at it.

FOURTH KID:
>Dryden steers it to the corner.

SECOND KID:
>Kharlamov has it again. He moves in on the net. He blasts it!

A new KID runs into the game.

FIFTH KID:
> Out of nowhere comes . . . Dave Kirk!

The FIFTH KID takes the ball.

FOURTH KID:
> Go, Davey, go!

FIFTH KID:
> He swings in front of his own net.

THIRD KID:
> Yayyyy, Davey!

FIFTH KID:
> He's up to the blueline.

FIRST KID:
> Less than a minute to go!

FIFTH KID:
> He cuts neatly back. He splits the defence. He's in on goal. He shoots, he scores!!!

THE KIDS:
> Yayyyyyyyy!

FIFTH KID:
> His teammates surround him!

FIRST KID:
> Davey, baby.

SECOND KID:
> Davey.

The ball meanwhile has bounced away.

THIRD KID:
> Hey, where's the puck?

> *It has gone towards KIRK.*

FIFTH KID:
> Hey, mister, will you throw us the ball?

> *They recognize him as DAVE KIRK, their hero.*

It's Dave Kirk!

> *They are in awe. He is embarrassed. They are all embarrassed.*

KIRK:
> Hey, even though you don't need us anymore, who's still . . . on the ice . . . not anywhere else, but on the *ice* . . . who's still number one?

THE KIDS: *puzzled, but responsive*
> Les Canadiens.

KIRK:
> Even though you don't need us.

THE KIDS:
> Les Canadiens!

KIRK:
> Even though it's just a game.

THE KIDS:
> Les Canadiens!

KIRK:
> Even though we're just a hockey team.

THE KIDS:
> LES CANADIENS!

KIRK: *to the ORGANIST*
Pierre . . .

THE ORGANIST:
Oui?

KIRK:
Joue ma chanson!

THE ORGANIST:
Avec plaisir, mon ami!

> *The ORGANIST begins playing "Les Canadiens sont là."*

Appendix

The following is a list, by page, of Engish translations to the French that appears in the text.

page 30

Maudits Anglais!

Fucking English bastards!

page 31

Maman t'attend à la maison.

Mama wants you home.

page 32

Ils sont jamais satisfait. L'Europe, l'Amérique. Maintenant le Canada.
Ici.

They're never satisfied. Europe, America. Now Canada.

Over here.

page 33

Cochons anglais!
Gérard, où es-tu?
T'es vivant?

English pigs!
Gerard, where are you?
You alive?

page 34

Non. Laisse-moi!
Il est ici.
Y dit qu' oui.
Crisse! Pourquoi?

No. Leave me!
He's here.
He says yes.
Christ! Why?

179

page 35

Quoi?

What?

page 36

Peux-tu l'attraper?
Y sont fous.

Can you catch?
They're crazy.

page 39

Tiens.

Here.

page 50

Georges, qu'est-ce que tu fais là maintenant?
Bonsoir mesdames et messieurs, et pour les Canadiens, Jacques Laviolette!

George, what are you up to there now?
Good evening ladies and gentlemen, and for the Canadiens, Jacques Laviolette!

page 64

Franchement, Léo, je trouve que tu exagères.
J'exagère? Il faut considérer la dimension historique.
Quelle dimension historique? Hey, il vient d'arriver en ville?
Evidemment.
Eh bien, il faut lui montrer quelque chose d'extraordinaire. Le Vieux Montréal. Le marché. Le coeur du frère André.
Quand il est ton invité, tu lui montres le coeur du frère André.

Frankly, Léo, I think you exaggerate.
I exaggerate? You have to consider the historical dimension.
What historical dimension? Hey, did he just get into town?
Obviously.
Well then, you've gotta show him something special. Old Montreal. The market. Brother André's pickled heart.
When he's your guest, you show him Brother André's heart.

page 73

Quel pauvre pays . . .

Poor country . . .

page 76

Est-ce que c'est la ligne pour les Canadiens?

Is this the line for the Canadiens' game?

page 77

Contre les Canadiens?
Les Canadiens aussi.
Il est fou des Canadiens.

Against the Canadiens?
Canadiens too.
He's crazy about the Canadiens.

page 80

Qu'est-ce que vous dites?   What?

page 83

Cent cinquante mille. $150,000.00.
Cent cinquante mille? Pour les $150,000.00? For the Canadiens?
Canadiens? Vendu!   Sold!

page 84

Bonsoir mesdames et messieurs,   Good evening ladies and gentle-
ici la voix des Canadiens avec   men, this is your voice of the
la joute de ce soir contre Tor-   Canadians, bringing you to-
onto. Et voici les joueurs qui   night's game against Toronto.
débuteront dans le match pours   Here are the starting lineups,
les Canadiens, et s'il vous plaît,   and please excuse my pronun-
excusez ma prononciation.   ciation.

page 85

Et maintenant, pour les Canadiens,   And now, for the Canadiens, it's
c'est . . . Wat-son qui essaie un   . . . Watson trying a pass.
relai.

page 86

Une série de déflections heroïques   A series of heroic stops by Bovier,
par Bovier, mais les Leafs ont   but the Leafs score. Down the
scoré. Y tombe sur la glace, c'est   ice, it's McMahon.
McMahon.
C'est écrit McMahon.   It's written McMahon.

page 88

T'sais qui gagne?   Who's winning?
Eux autres. C'est même pas fini.   Them. It's not even over. Eight
Huit à un.   one.

page 89

T'sais qui a compté?   Who got the goal?
O'Connor, sur une passe de   O'Connor, on a pass from Getliffe
Getliffe et Watson.   and Watson.
O'Conner, puis Getliffe, Watson?   O'Connor, then Getliffe, Watson?
J'ai une offre à jouer à Trois-   I got an offer to play at Trois
Rivières.   Rivières.
Une autre?   A new one?
J'y pense.   I'm thinking about it.
Toi-là, tu restes, puis tu finis tes   You stay and finish school.
études.

Pourquoi c'est faire? Les mathé-matiques? L'anglais?
Arrête-moi ça.

For what? Mathematics? English?
Come on.

page 94

A bas la conscription.

Down with Conscription.

page 123

Bonjour, la classe. Asseyez-vous. Comme vous pouvez voir, je ne suis pas votre professeur régulier. Aujourd'hui nous ne suivons pas la routine.
Ce n'est pas une journée ordinaire. C'est une journée *extra*ordin-aire. Extraordinaire! Mademoi-selle Chapleau, votre professeur régulier . . . Mademoiselle Chap-leau? L'autre professeur?
Oui. Mademoiselle Chapleau est allée faire son devoir.

Good morning, class. Sit down. As you can see, I am not your regular teacher. Today we are not following the usual routine.

This is not an ordinary day. It is an *extra*ordinary day. Extra-ordinary! Miss Chapleau, your regular teacher . . . Miss Chap-leau? The other teacher?

Yes. Miss Chapleau has gone to vote.

page 124

Le morceau de papier. Le petit "eeks." Plier le papier. Et dans la boîte.
Oui, monsieur. Elle est allée faire son devoir. Je suis Mademoiselle Miron.
Eh bien, messieurs. C'est une drôle de place pour une classe de français. Une drôle de place? . . .

The piece of paper. The little "x." Fold the paper. And into the box.
Yes, sir. She went to vote. I am Miss Miron.

Well, gentlemen. This is a strange place for a French class. A strange place? . . .

page 125

Enfin, j'ai enseigné un peu par-tout. Voyons. Votre dernière classe était . . . il y a trois semaines! C'est une assez longue absence pour des gens à un niveau si primitif! Et avant ça, encore deux semaines! Laissez-moi vous dire messieurs, si vous ne pouvez pas venir en classe dans une manière plus régulière, je ne peux pas voir comment vous allez pouvoir maîtriser le le belle langue de Molière!

Still, I've taught in many settings. Look. Your last class was . . . three weeks ago! That's quite a long absence for people at such a primitive level! And before that, another two weeks? Let me say, gentlemen, that if you can't come to class more regu-larly, I don't see how you'll ever be able to master the beautiful language of Molière!

182

Excusez-moi, monsieur, mais quand nous sommes en classe, je regrette de ne pas pouvoir comprendre un seul mot de ce que vous dites. Pas un mot. Notre première regle: le français seulement. Mais si vous voulez nous expliquer en français quelle est la nature de votre problème, ça serait utile à tous et à toute.

Excuse me, sir, but while we are in class, I'm afraid I can't understand a word of what you're saying. Not a word. Our first rule: French only. But if you want to explain in French what the problem is, that could be very useful to all of us.

Nous travaillons dans Montréal.
Oui, monsieur, allez-y!
Et aussi nous travaillons . . .

We work in Montreal.
Yes, sir, go ahead!
And we also work . . .

page 126

Tout le monde.
Et alors?
Nous allons toujours . . .
Souvent.
A une autre place. A des autres places.

Everybody.
So?
We always go . . .
Often.
To another place. To other places.

Mes pauvres étudiants. Si c'est trop difficile pour vous de m'expliquer pourquoir vous ne pouvez pas venir en classe d'une manière plus régulière, peut-être vous pouvez m'expliquer pourquoi vous voulez apprendre le français de toute façon. Eh?

My poor students. If it strains you so much to tell me why you can't come to class regularly, maybe you can explain why you want to bother learning French at all. Eh?

page 127

Pourquoi-voulez-vous-apprendre-le-français? Vous, monsieur?
Il y a des garçons . . . des autres garçons . . . avec nous . . .
Garçons?
Nous travaillons avec des gars qui parlent anglais à nous. Et nous voulons parler français à . . . à . . . à . . .
Ah-ah-ah, monsieur. En français. Qu'est-ce que c'est? A . . . à . . .

Why do you want to learn French? You, sir?
There are some boys . . . some other boys . . . with us . . .
Boys?
We work with guys who speak English to us. And we want to speak French to . . . to . . . to . . .
No, no, no. In French. What is it? To . . . to . . .

page 128

Mais qui êtes-vous donc? Des freaks du bilinguisme?

So what are you then? Bilingualism freaks?

page 129

Il faut vouloir apprendre le français.

You have to want to learn French.

Monsieur, comme je vous ai dit, je ne comprends pas un seul mot de ce que vous dites.

Sir, as I said, I don't understand a single word that you say.

Ah, la fameuse "unité nationale!"

Oh, yes, the famous "national unity!"

page 130

Très bien, monsieur!

Very good!

page 131

Mes joueurs ont tous des beaux patins . . .

My players have all fine skates . . .

page 131

Des belles bretelles!
Un chandail propre!
Des beaux bas blancs!
Des bonnes jambieres!
Des épaulettes!
Des beaux patins!

Suspenders!
Sweater!
White socks!
Kneepads!
Shoulder pads!
Skates!

page 140

Hey, regarde qui dort à la switch. Les deux souris aveugles.

Hey, look who's asleep at the switch. The two blind mice.

Oh-ho, le buffon de Chicoutimi.

Ho, ho, it's the old horse thief from Chicoutimi.

page143

Appelez-moi Lise!

Call me Lise!

page 144

Au secours . . .
Fini!

Help . . .
That's all!

page 145

Ecoutez, n'écrivez pas!

Listen, don't write!

page 152

Salut, les gars.

Hi, guys.

page 157

Henri, c'est vrai qu' tu'as écrit c' t'article-là?

Henry, did you really write it?

Qui d'autre?

Who else?

page 170

A partir d'aujourd'hui, demain nous appartient,

From today on, tomorrow is ours,

Un pays aujourd'hui si vraiment on y tient . . .

A national today if we really want it . . .

C'est un miracle!

It's a miracle!

C' pas vrai. Dis-moi que c' pas vrai.

It isn't true. Tell me it isn't true.

Combien de sièges maintenant?

How many seats now?

Soixante-huit!

Sixty-eight!

Hey, c'est fini dans Mercier.

It's over in Mercier riding.

T'sais qui a gagné?

Who won?

Godin. Bourassa yé chomeur!

Godin. Bourassa is out of work!

page 171

On a gagne tout! Tout le monde a gagné!

We won everything! Everybody won!

Gagné!

Won!

Oui. Gagné. Quatre à deux dans le match.

Yeah. Won. Four to two in the game.

Soixante-huit à trente-trois!

Sixty-eight to thirty-three!

Hey, hey, en français!

Uh-uh, French only!

Hey, viens-tu au Paul Sauvé avec nous autres?

Hey, are you coming to the Paul Sauvé Arena with us?

page 172

Lévesque va faire un discours.

Lévesque will be making a speech.

Non, ch' peux pas. J'ai pas de babysitter.

I can't I haven't got a babysitter.

On y va.

Let's go.

page 178

Joue ma chanson!

Play my song!

Avec plaisir, mon ami!

With pleasure, my friend!

The text photographs are from the Toronto Workshop Production of Les Canadiens. The actors featured in them, by page from left to right, are as follows:

page 26

Len Doncheff, Sebastien Dhavernas, Jeff Braunstein, Raymond Belisle, Johnathan Welsh and Bill Lake.

page 37
Suzette Couture and Raymond Belisle.

page 38
Sebastien Dhavernas.

page 53
Sebastien Dhavernas, Bill Lake, Johnathan Welsh and Jeff Braunstein.

page 54
Suzette Couture and Sebastien Dhavernas.

page 61
Bill Lake.

page 62
Pierre Lenoir and Bill Lake.

page 95
Raymond Belisle.

page 96
Jeff Braunstein, Len Doncheff, Johnathan Welsh, Raymond Belisle, Bill Lake and Sebastien Dhavernas.

186